KEEPING

700 YEARS OF CATHOLIC LIFE IN HULL

Edited by

JOHN MARKHAM

Highgate of Beverley
Highgate Publications (Beverley) Ltd.
1999

British Library Cataloguing in Publication Data.
A catalogue record for this book is available from the British Library.

© 1999

All authors retain the copyright of their individual articles and assert the moral right
to be identified as the authors of the work included in this book.

ISBN 1 902645 08 1

Published by

Highgate of Beverley

Highgate Publications (Beverley) Limited
4 Newbegin, Lairgate, Beverley, HU17 8EG. Telephone (01482) 886017

Produced by

ba/*print*

4 Newbegin, Lairgate, Beverley, HU17 8EG. Telephone (01482) 886017

Front Cover Picture: St. Charles Borromeo, Hull (Stephen Robinson).

Back Cover: Church of the Augustinian Friars, Blackfriargate (Kingston upon Hull City Council).

Title Page: St. Charles Borromeo, Hull (Stephen Robinson).

Contents

Illustrations

Notes on Contributors

Janet Doyle   An honours graduate in History of Durham University. Taught for many years in Hull schools. Now very active in voluntary and church work. Currently Treasurer of the Northern Credit Union and Chair of the Hull and District Catholic Pastoral Council.

Patrick J. Doyle   An honours graduate in History and M.A. of Durham University. Awarded honorary doctorates by Hull University and the University of Lincolnshire and Humberside. Former college and university lecturer in History. Elected to Hull City Council 1972; Leader since 1979.

Barbara English   A graduate of the University of St. Andrews. Worked as an archivist and in publishing. Joined the staff of Hull University 1979. Now Emeritus Professor of History. Publications include *The Lords of Holderness 1086-1260* and *The Great Landowners of East Yorkshire 1830-1910*.

Jo Gibbons (née Nelson)   A native of Hull with a lifelong interest in local history. Educated at St. Mary's Grammar School and is a parishioner of St. Anthony's church. Gained her bachelor's and master's degrees as a part-time student at the University of Lincolnshire and Humberside where she is presently employed as a Senior Administrative Officer.

David Grant was born in Hull in 1957. He studied for the priesthood at Ushaw College and the University of Durham prior to ordination at the Sacred Heart Church, Hull, in 1982. Since 1996 he has been the Parish priest of Marton and Hornsea.

Marie McClelland   A graduate of the National University of Ireland and of Hull University. Head teacher of St. Oswald's and St. Anne's Primary School, Hull. Has lectured and written on Catholic history in 19th-century Hull.

John Markham   A graduate of Hull University with an M.A. and Diploma in Local Historical Studies. Formerly a principal lecturer at what is now the University of Lincolnshire and Humberside and currently a lecturer and consultant for Vista (East Yorkshire Adult Courses). A writer and publisher.

Peter Stubley   Until recently was a chaplain with the North Humberside Industrial Mission and a part-time lecturer at the University of Hull, Department of Theology. Author of *A House Divided: Evangelicals and the Establishment in Hull 1770-1914.*

J. Anthony Williams, M.A., B.Sc.(Econ.), F.S.A., F.R.Hist.Soc. Principal Lecturer in History at Endsleigh College of Education, Hull. Has served on Middlesbrough Diocesan ecumenical commission and as a governor of Hull Catholic schools. Author of works on many aspects of Catholic History.

Editor's Introduction

This book has been produced in 1999, the year of the celebrations entitled Hull 700, as a timely record of the contribution made by the Catholic Church and by individual Catholics to the history of Hull in the 700 years which have passed since the grant of its first charter in 1299.

I was invited by Patrick Doyle to edit a collection of articles by writers who were all experts in their fields. My other brief was to prepare the biographies of some prominent Hull Catholics as well as 'filling in the gaps' which this type of publication tends to leave. This is not, and has never been envisaged as, the comprehensive and definitive history of Catholicism in Hull, which remains to be written. Yet, in view of its pragmatic structure, there are perhaps fewer lacunae than might have been expected. Many subjects deserve fuller treatment in future publications, and the emphasis is certainly on the history of the period since Emancipation in 1829. But overall the total coverage of the contributors, who have worked quite independently, has resulted in a picture of Catholicism in Hull which is not blatantly unfair or unbalanced. Not all the authors are Catholics, and, although the general tone is sympathetic, this work has neither been intended nor prepared as a proselytising publication.

In the early years of Hull's existence, the Catholic Church was an integral part of the town's life and the secular and ecclesiastical were closely inter-related. Janet Doyle has set the opening scene with her article on the coming of Christianity to the area, the Rev. David Grant has described the foundation and history of the religious orders in medieval Hull, and Professor Barbara English has written of the Pilgrimage of Grace, the failed attempt to restore the Church to its pre-Reformation structure and practices. After J. Anthony Williams' article on the events in the 18th and early 19th centuries, the focus is on the influx of Irish immigrants, Catholic progress and anti-Catholic prejudice, the first Mercy nuns in Hull and the position of Catholics in the context of a largely Protestant population, with articles by Jo Gibbons, Marie McClelland and the Rev. Dr. Peter Stubley, while Patrick Doyle continues the story to the present time.

The very active Hull press from 1794 onwards helps to fill in the gaps and to reinforce points made in the body of the work. With some judicious reading between the lines it is possible to capture a hint of the atmosphere of religious life in Hull, a mood more elusive and less easy to convey than factual information. No one would ever hope to write a full and accurate history based purely on press sources, for what is important is not necessarily considered newsworthy, and newspapers tend to over-state differences and to heighten controversy. Nevertheless, though Hull newspapers had their undisguised religious stance, this obvious bias is much easier to identify and discount than the pretended objectivity of some modern publications

One fact, whatever a newspaper's viewpoint, is immediately obvious: the centrality of religion and its consequent role as a major issue in political debate. As well as Emancipation, the restoration of the hierarchy, the Maynooth grant, Church tithes, the disestablishment of the Church of Ireland (later the constitutional position of Ireland itself), and the funding of schools all featured prominently in electoral controversy, while clergymen made their own affiliations public by sitting on political platforms. 'No Popery' cries were common for a large part of the 19th century, and religion could be a minefield for parliamentary candidates, who had to satisfy forceful Protestant pressure groups of their own unwavering commitment to Protestantism by answering a list of key questions in the knowledge that the 'right' reply was important to the success of their campaigns. On occasions one is aware of the struggle they were having with their consciences in order to avoid compromising their more tolerant and broad-minded attitudes.

Anti-Catholic prejudice is undeniable and, as Dr. Stubley shows, it was vividly demonstrated in the speeches and petitioning aroused by the imminence of Emancipation. Even those attacks on the proposed reform, however (with some notable exceptions), frequently made a distinction between the right of Catholics to practise their own religion and their unsuitability to exercise political power. In contrast to the pre-Reformation period, when the Church was integrated into English life, by the 19th century it was seen as a foreign institution, hostile to the civil liberties enjoyed by Englishmen since the Glorious Revolution of 1688. The passing of time was needed to prove that both the Old and Young Pretenders belonged to the past and that granting full civil rights to Catholics proved no threat to either the monarchy or the revered Constitution.

The Hull-born campaigner against slavery, William Wilberforce, was typical of many who saw a danger in the political power of Catholics, but he had the magnanimity and generosity of mind to accept the unfairness of Catholic disabilities in Ireland and to conclude that Catholic Members of Parliament would not be so great an evil.

When a mass meeting, called to consider petitioning Parliament against Catholic Emancipation, was held in Hull's Market Place on 2 March 1829, appropriately in front of the statue of William III, speaker after speaker fulminated against the intolerance and habitual cruelty inherent in Catholicism. 'When Protestants persecute it is contrary to their principles,' said the Rev. John Scott, the Evangelical vicar of St. Mary's, Lowgate, 'but when Roman Catholics persecute it is in conformity with their principles . . . On this account the more sincere a Roman Catholic is, the more he is to be dreaded.' Edward Gibson, a shipowner, appealed to Hull parents to safeguard the liberties of generations yet unborn: 'When your bodies shall be laid in your graves, and your flesh shall mingle with its kindred earth, O give not your children power to lift up the finger of scorn and, pointing to your blotted escutcheon, to say, "My father was one that helped to mar the Constitution of this country." ' But in the midst of these denunciations, even he claimed to make a distinction between religious and political rights: 'Sorry should I be to possess unchristian feelings towards my Roman Catholic brethren. If the petitions which have just been read contained one sentiment that involved their right to public or private worship, I, for one, should not support them.'

A particular target for abuse was Daniel Sykes, a Whig M.P. for Hull, who presented in the Commons a petition from the Unitarians 'stating the inalienable right of everyone to worship God according to his conscience, without the intervention of any law inflicting punishment or creating disabilities'. Quantifying and analysing public opinion, particularly when it is influenced with strong emotion, instinctive reactions and atavistical attitudes, is difficult enough when psephological methods are applied to current events. Assessing the views of Hull residents of 1829 is fraught with greater problems, and one's conclusions are often a subjective interpretation of what evidence is available. Certainly Daniel Sykes believed that the vocal agitators who organised anti-Catholic petitions and participated in public debate were not representative of the vast majority.

A petition presented earlier by his fellow M.P., Augustus O'Neill, against Catholic claims, did not, he said, 'proceed from any public meeting, but, as he had been informed since he came to town, had been laid at some shops, and persons, something like the "barkers" at mock auctions, invited the passengers in the street to walk in and subscribe their name. These, he believed, amounted to only some hundreds out of a population of 45,000, and therefore could only be taken as expressing the wishes of that small proportion of the population of Hull . . . He was inclined to think that there was not an universal hostile feeling to the Catholics of Hull, from considering that he had twice been chosen to represent that populous borough, though at all times, and in all places, whenever a fair opportunity has presented, he had openly avowed his opinion that concession of the Catholic claims was a measure of justice and policy at all times, and lately one of necessity.' Nevertheless, these anti-Catholic campaigners were now able to undermine Sykes' support in Hull so successfully that, in order to remain an M.P., in 1830 he felt obliged to abandon his Hull constituency for Beverley.

Emancipation did not result in the destruction of the British Constitution which the speakers in the Market Place so confidently forecast, but passions were stirred again by the restoration of the hierarchy in 1850, and particularly by the title, Bishop of Beverley, granted to the former Vicar Apostolic, Dr. John Briggs. In November 1850, 70 East Riding clergymen, predominantly Low Church in outlook, met in Beverley to protest against this act of 'Papal aggression' in which it was alleged an Italian bishop claimed to have control over affairs within the Queen's realm. On this occasion the son of the Vicar of St. Mary's, Lowgate, who had spoken so vehemently against Emancipation, and who bore his father's name, John Scott, was unambiguous in his condemnation of 'the extraordinary and momentous character of the Papal movement' and 'those strange doctrines which, he regretted to say, had not only found their way into, but had taken deep root within, the Church [of England]'. Ironically, his own son, yet another John Scott, was to become a leading Anglo-Catholic. St. Mary's, Lowgate, where he followed his forebears as vicar, was to establish itself as a High Church stronghold and to maintain that tradition ever since. Archdeacon Robert Wilberforce, who had convened the meeting at the request of his clerics (but who gave a somewhat sophisticated explanation of his own absence), was received into the Catholic Church four years later.

The *cause célèbre* of the Rev. Henry Astrop, a member of a Hull merchant family and the first resident priest in Beverley, who married in Sutton parish church in 1852 and fathered a child, provided a colourful story for the press and excellent ammunition for anti-Catholics, with one forceful Protestant activist, the Rev. Dr. John E. Armstrong, holding a monster meeting in Hull, conducting a vigorous campaign by placards and instigating a petition to Queen Victoria on the grounds that Father Astrop, who soon repented of his misdeeds and retired to a religious house in Bruges, was a British citizen taken into bondage by Catholic priests. There was understandable sympathy from everyone for Mrs. Astrop, who was left in a tragic situation, and Dean Trappes of St. Charles dealt diplomatically and sensitively with the agonising problem of a priest in an acute state of mental conflict and the abandoned wife, who resorted to violence in an attempt to obtain the justice she felt she had been denied. Perhaps one's surprise is not that the affair made news, but that interest evaporated so quickly and left no trace in public memory.

Even before Archdeacon Wilberforce's conversion, Hull had witnessed the resignation in 1851 of two popular curates of Holy Trinity. The *Hull Advertiser*, an untiring opponent of all forms of intolerance and bigotry under the editorship of E. F. Collins, printed in full the last sermon, a moving *apologia proita sua*, preached by the Rev. T. S. Barff, which was listened to with breathless attention by the large congregation which was assembled, 'many being affected even to tears'. The *Advertiser* also published a long, painful letter from the second resigning curate, the Rev. Thomas Dykes, who denied that he had ever spoken with anything but the greatest affection and respect about his grandfather, the distinguished Evangelical clergyman, the Rev. T. B. Dykes, and asked only to be 'as bold and uncompromising in support of what my conscience tells me is right as he was'. It was, though, tactless for Thomas Dykes to return to Hull as a Jesuit a few years later to assist at a mission at St. Charles.

Outbursts of anti-Catholic prejudice, often irritating and unpleasant, though not too serious, continued to surface from time to time. In 1861, for example, two nuns were reported as having been insulted in the street by men acting under the influence of anti-Catholic lecturers, while in 1869 the Rev. Bernard Randerson complained to the Guardians of the Sculcoates Union about 'the difficulties that Catholic children have to contend with in a workhouse', and about insults directed at himself. As he was passing a group of children, 'one of the boys took hold of a Catholic boy, and, pointing to me, shouted, "Forgive us our sins, twopence a dozen." ' On two other occasions he had been shouted at and subjected to 'a general hubbub'. Father Randerson did point out that he was making no complaint against the master, 'who has afforded me every opportunity of visiting the Catholic inmates'. Hostility to Catholics was, like most prejudice, a consequence of vague and often inaccurate knowledge, or complete ignorance, of history. From the poorer people, who had to live cheek by jowl with immigrants of a different culture and compete with them for jobs, some resentment was only to be expected, but the verbal attacks at the time of the great controversies were made by educated and articulate laymen and clerics who saw religious issues through the distorting lenses of sectarian spectacles and kept controversy alive until commonsense or indifference prevailed.

Yet, in spite of so much evidence, it is fair to conclude that public debates and press coverage were not always true reflections of attitudes and behaviour displayed in everyday situations. Protestants who disliked the image of the Catholic Church and what they imagined it taught may well have found that individual Catholics were as normal as themselves. Friendship and kindness may have flourished more strongly than official disputes and pronouncements suggested. The number of Catholics who made successful careers is at least some evidence that those of ability could prosper in spite of what appears to be a hostile environment.

To quote the Unitarian industrialist, Henry Blundell, when he complained about the sectarian warfare imported into the general election of 1852: 'It is the clergy of Hull who have caused this political strife. If they had kept to their proper places as ministers of the gospel and left the Reformers and the respectable Conservatives to settle affairs, I believe there would have been nothing to set the whole town by the ears . . .'

Through the kindness of Martin Craven, who is not only a local historian but also an enthusiastic collector, I have been privileged to look at Catholic miscellanea he has acquired over the years. Varied and haphazard as these items are, they are invaluable in filling some of the gaps left between specialist articles on specific subjects. The picture which emerges in the late 19th and early 20th centuries is of a close-knit community which rallied round in support of fund-raising and religious and social events.

An elaborately conceived three-day bazaar, 'Killarney in Hull', where all the stalls were decorated to represent Irish scenes, was held at the Artillery Barracks in November 1905, its aim to reduce the 'huge debt of over £5,000' on the new St. Patrick's church. The souvenir programme produced for the occasion has gained historical value over the past nine decades by placing on record the names of those who contributed their time and efforts to making the event a success. The mundane lists of committee members include surnames which recur elsewhere and which serve as a modest tribute to their work for the Church. The first day was opened by Edward Dixon, the second by Sir Henry Seymour King, the M.P. for Central Hull, and the third day by Mrs. T. F. Farrell. An advertisement in the programme refers to two publications issued from 26 Charlotte Street: the *Hull Catholic Herald* and the *Catholic Home Journal*.

There was still sufficient debt outstanding for another three-day bazaar in 1910, this time on the theme of Abbeys, and the venue the Assembly Rooms. Once again there was a judicious mixture of Catholic and non-Catholic personalities, with the first-day opener, Lady Herries, the second, Miss Muriel Wilson, a member of the great shipping family of Tranby Croft, and the third, the Sheriff, Mr. E. Dumoulin.

Lengthy scholarly introductions were provided in these programmes by Edmund Wrigglesworth, who also acted as a secretary, and whose name occurs so often that one realises that he was a leading member of Hull's Catholic community. Although his name is not generally known, he was obviously a pioneering local historian of considerable ability with a pen which was not allowed to remain idle for long. His best-known work is Brown's *Illustrated Guide to Hull*, published in 1891 and reprinted in recent years, a book which includes some extremely useful information on Hull's buildings and organisations at the turn of the century. His output included other now rare books, *Beverley's Roll of Honour, History's Romance, Kingston-upon-Hull, Past and Present* and a booklet, *List of Books by Catholic Writers in the Hull Public Libraries*. Articles on 'Ancient Gilds' were published in *The Rosary*, and on 'The Curiosities of Horology' and 'Curious Watches' in *The Catholic Children's Magazine*. There are probably many more waiting to be located.

Another interesting item in Martin Craven's collection is *A Short History of Hull Circle 7 of the Catenian Association*, produced to commemorate the 1,000th meeting on 28 June 1996 of the organisation founded in 1911 in response to a petition to the Grand Circle from Ambrose Dowling, Manice Ambrose Regan, Pierce Joseph Tucker, Joseph Chapman, Edmund Wrigglesworth, E. F. C. Forster, and R. Galloway. Catholicism in England had been sustained by the Old Catholic families and later substantially enlarged by the influx of working-class Irish people. The Catenians recognised that middle-class Catholics were a growing section of society, and their members were encouraged to take places on public committees, councils and the bench, and by their punctilious behaviour to help dispel any anti-Catholic bias which persisted.

The short history records the problems of world wars when the Catenians of Hull struggled to survive in the most difficult circumstances. Meetings moved from the Royal Station Hotel to Powolny's restaurant and later to the Catholic Central Club, 317 Beverley Road, before transferring to the Imperial Hotel, Paragon Street.

In its early years two distinguished members died as a result of war and, indirectly, its aftermath, Bede Farrell and Sir Mark Sykes, while Brother Manice A. Regan, who had served as a Commander in the R.N.V.R., was awarded the O.B.E. At one meeting the ever-active Edmund Wrigglesworth read a paper on 'English Life in the Middle Ages as illustrated in the History of Holy Trinity Church, Hull', and highlights of later years included a dinner in 1925 at the Guildhall at the express invitation of the non-Catholic Lord Mayor, and a similar event at the same venue in 1936 attended by Dr. Arthur Hinsley, Archbishop of Westminster.

The Second World War brought problems to a number, not least B. G. Conlon, whose premises were blitzed twice and his home ruined. W. Morris, as City Engineer, organised Civil Defence and Rescue Services for the City and was awarded the O.B.E.

Tributes were paid in the history to long-standing members, among them J. H. Sutcliffe, A. H. Moses, C. J. Collingwood, Thomas Rafferty, Hubert Rafferty, W. G. Nevin, Herbert Conlon, Arthur Brunner (brother of George, Bishop of Middlesbrough) and B. McKenna.

The world has changed dramatically since 1911 and the Catenians have reflected this social revolution. 'Because of the good work done by their predecessors,' states the history, 'they no longer spend time exploring the means of getting Catholics on public committees and councils.' Such a conclusion provides in a few words a significant commentary on Catholic life in Hull and a concise addendum to the subjects which the contributors have discussed in their separate articles.

September 1999   John Markham

East Yorkshire Anglo-Saxon Saints and Scholars

by
Janet Doyle

Our English forefathers arrived in Britain in the fifth and sixth centuries, invaders from the Continent, from Germany, the Low Countries and Denmark, a mixed group of Angles, Saxons, Jutes, Franks and Frisians, usually known collectively as Anglo-Saxons. They were Teutonic people of a different racial group and language from the Celtic British tribes who inhabited this island from before the Roman occupation; in these days of the European Union, perhaps we should be more conscious of our Continental origins.

The end of the Roman Empire saw people on the move, with the Franks taking over Gaul and the English coming to Britain. Our ancestors came gradually, at first as mercenaries who settled peacefully, but then increasingly as hostile invaders, conquering the country from its British owners. The British fought hard and it was a bitter, protracted struggle, but by 600 England as we know it today was under English control, with the British only retaining Wales and the Devon-Cornwall peninsula, although the latter would eventually fall to the newcomers. Many British princes and landowners were driven out or killed, but unknown numbers of ordinary people stayed under new masters. In time the British became known as the Welsh, and the enmity and division between them and the English invaders was naturally very deep. For some 400 years the British had been proud to be part of the Roman Empire and were Christians, converted as Christianity spread through the Empire. The English were barbarians from outside the Empire and pagans into the bargain, facts which widened the gulf, and the British felt no obligation to try and convert their enemies.

Anglo-Saxon England was divided into several small kingdoms or principalities, among which were Kent, Wessex, East Anglia, Mercia and Northumbria, often squabbling and fighting with each other. Hull lay in Northumbria, the kingdom north of the great geographical boundary of

Goodmanham Church. (Stephen Robinson)

the River Humber, and, although Hull as such did not exist at this time, there were settlements at Myton, Wyke and Cottingham. Beverley was an established English town, and we know that either Barton or Barrow on the south bank had an early monastry founded by St. Chad. Barton church has a fine Anglo-Saxon tower. Goodmanham in the East Riding had a pagan temple and lay in the vicinity of one of the royal estates. Here was enacted, on our doorstep, a momentous and dramatic piece of history. In 627 King Edwin of Northumbria called his council together at Goodmanham to decide whether his kingdom should become Christian. St. Augustine had landed in Kent 30 years earlier, in 597, and begun the conversion of the English, events celebrated in frescoes in the sanctuary of St. Charles church. King Edwin's queen, Ethelberga, was a Kentish princess, whose brother had allowed the marriage on condition that she could practise her faith and bring a bishop with her, namely Paulinus, one of Augustine's fellow missionaries. Pope Boniface wrote encouraging letters to the King and Queen, urging Ethelberga to use her influence to convert her husband, and Edwin to accept Christianity and 'inherit eternal life'. After a dramatic incident, when his best friend, Lilla, threw himself between the King and an assassin and was killed, Edwin allowed the baby daughter born that same day to be baptised.

We are more than fortunate to possess a vivid account of these events in St. Bede's *History of the English Church and People*. This Northumbrian monk, born in 673, confessor and doctor of the church, a man of profound scholarship and a wonderful teacher, whose work is still eminently readable today, speaks to us across the centuries. He paints exquisite cameos of the men and women of his time, and, conscious that he was living at a watershed of history, strove to preserve the story of the forging of his nation and its conversion to Christianity. To him the preaching of the gospel and the salvation of souls in a pagan world was paramount.

Bede says that Edwin abandoned the worship of idols, but he wanted 'to discuss his proper course with his chief counsellors, on whose wisdom he placed great reliance. For the King was by nature a wise and prudent man, and often sat alone in silence for long periods, turning over in his mind what he should do, and which religion he should follow'. Edwin was watching the reactions of his nobles to the new religion. Royal power was extensive, but a king would be unwise to upset his chief men, whom he relied on to fight for him in battle. If they had been hostile to Christianity, it would have been very difficult for the King to convert, but the English do not seem to have been particularly staunch in their paganism. When a ruler was converted, then the nobles followed, and ordinary people had little choice in the matter – they obeyed their masters. Ideas of individual conscience and choice were then quite foreign to society.

At the Goodmanham Council the King asked everyone in turn to give their opinion of the new faith. People were in favour of conversion, even Coifi, the pagan High Priest, who said that, 'the religion we have hitherto professed seems valueless and powerless'. He added: 'None of your subjects has been more devoted to the service of the gods than myself, yet there are many to whom you show greater favour' – a practical if somewhat selfish argument. A much more thoughtful contribution came from one man who said: 'Your Majesty, when we compare the present life of man with that time of which we have no knowledge, it seems to me like the swift flight of a lone sparrow through the banqueting hall where you sit in the winter months to dine with your thanes (nobles) and counsellors. Inside there is a comforting fire to warm the room, outside the wintry storms of snow and rain are raging. This sparrow flies swiftly in through one door of the hall and out through another. While he is inside, he is safe from the winter storms, but, after a few moments of comfort, he vanishes from sight into the darkness whence he came. Similarly, man appears on earth for a little while, but we know nothing of what went before this life, and what follows. Therefore if this new teaching can reveal any more certain knowledge, it seems only right that we should follow it.'

And so the Northumbrians embraced Christianity. Coifi himself volunteered to be the first to profane the pagan shrines, and, bearing arms, he galloped off on a stallion, things forbidden to a high priest, who was only supposed to ride a mare and not carry weapons. The locals at Goodmanham were astounded to see him pound up to their temple, throw his spear into it and order it to be fired: 'they thought he had gone mad'. There are stained glass windows in the lovely Norman church at Goodmanham commemorating these events, and the church itself, although not Anglo-Saxon, undoubtedly stands on the same site as the pagan temple. King Edwin was baptised at York on Easter Day in the eleventh year of his reign, and Bishop Paulinus worked ceaselessly, teaching and baptising, sometimes in the open air in rivers, throughout the kingdom.

Sadly the story does not end happily. Six years later Edwin was killed in battle by King Penda of Mercia, and Paulinus and the Queen had to flee to the safety of Kent, where Paulinus became Bishop of Rochester. The work of conversion fell to other hands. Northumbria descended into chaos for a time, until another branch of the royal family gained control of the kingdom under the saintly King Oswald, and Irish monks led by St. Aidan took up the task of evangelisation from Holy Island. The Roman Mission in the south of England, after some initial success, experienced difficulties and was limited in scope, and undoubtedly it was the Irish who provided the manpower and the zeal for the conversion of England. Irish monks impressed the English, as did Augustine's, with their simple life-style, putting into practice what they preached. In marked contrast to the rich and powerful of their day, they did not carry weapons, wore clothes rather like the ordinary peasant, lived in simple buildings, and yet were educated, respected men, who influenced kings and political events. It was a recipe for missionary success.

The organisation of the early church in England was monastic, that is to say, before there were parish churches, monasteries large and small were founded, acting as 'mission centres', very busy places, part village, part farm, part school, part seminary, from which the monks moved out to evangelise the surrounding countryside, teaching, baptising, saying Mass, until gradually over the years parish churches were endowed and built. Bishops were itinerant, constantly on the move with the clerics of their household, leading the missionary work, going from monastery to monastery, using them as bases for work in the villages, with a favourite monastery acting as a retreat house where they could recharge their batteries, like Lindisfarne for St. Aidan and Beverley for our own St. John. Lastingham was an important local monastery, founded by St. Cedd, Bishop of the East Saxons, who dedicated the site with a rigorous fast during Lent.

He died of plague and was buried there in 659; the interesting Anglo-Saxon crypt survives. Cedd was the brother of St. Chad, both of whom were bishops, and they had two more brothers who were priests, 'a rare occurrence in one family', as Bede remarks.

It is to John of Beverley that we will now turn, for information about him shows Christianity spreading outwards from Beverley into our locality. He was, according to tradition, born at Harpham in the East Riding, where there is still a well known as St. John's Well. He entered Whitby Abbey, a double monastery containing both monks and nuns, an interesting and peculiarly English institution, where he trained under its great founder, St. Hilda.

Another four of her monks as well as John became bishops – quite an achievement. He seems to have spent some time in the south working under Theodore, Archbishop of Canterbury, because Bede recounts him

saying, 'I remember that Archbishop Theodore, of blessed memory said . . .' John was made bishop of Hexham in 685, according to the Anglo-Saxon Chronicle, though it may have been a little later, and he was translated to York in 705. He ordained Bede both deacon and priest, so it is fitting that Bede should devote several affectionate chapters of his history to his own bishop, getting much of his information from Berthun 'a truthful man, formerly John's deacon and now abbot of the monastery known as "Inderawood", which means "In the wood of the Deiri".' All the evidence suggests that Inderawood and Beverley are one and the same.

Statue of St. John of Beverley in Beverley Minster. (Stephen Robinson)

John was bishop for 33 years, retiring to his monastery at Inderawood near the end of his life, when 'his advanced years prevented him from administering his bishopric'. His death in 721, when he must have been well into his 70s, was also recorded in the Anglo-Saxon Chronicle, a tribute to his fame and saintliness: 'In this year passed away the holy Bishop John, who was bishop thirty-three years, eight months and thirteen days: his body rests at Beverley.' And there he still lies, within the present great Minster, which is hallowed by his presence. The Catholic church at Beverley is dedicated to him, and there are statues of him, together with Bede, Hilda, and Paulinus in St. Charles church, tributes to an array of wonderful local saints.

Bede's stories show John as a man of great common-sense and compassion as well as holiness. The best known concerns a 'dumb youth'. The Bishop had an isolated house near Hexham, which he used for retreats especially in Lent, and one year he took an interest in a poor, local, dumb youth with 'so many scabs and scales on his head that no hair ever grew on the crown, but only a few wisps in a ragged circle'. The kindly but shrewd Bishop noticed that, although the boy could not speak he could hear: presumably he had been born deaf but his hearing had returned. John summoned the youth to him, examined his mouth and tongue, and, finding no physical impediment, proceeded to give him speech therapy every day, starting with the sounds of the alphabet, 'A B C'. The boy learnt to speak – personal attention from the Bishop himself was probably a great incentive. Bede calls this a miracle, but he used the term more loosely than we do. The Bishop's doctor also managed to clear the boy's scabby head with creams, and his hair grew properly. It is a lovely story. John offered to take the lad into his household, but he preferred to go back to his family, an interesting example of how the church could offer ordinary people an education and open up to them an alternative life and career.

Other incidents took place near Hull. John visited a convent of nuns at Wetadun (Watton) in the East Riding, where the abbess begged him to see one of the nuns, her own daughter, who was very ill, 'being sure that she would improve if the Bishop blessed or touched her'. The Bishop was most unwilling to be used in this way. 'What can I do for the girl if she is going to die?' he said. However, he was finally persuaded, said a prayer and blessed the girl, and – she recovered that very evening. Her mother intended her to become the next abbess, which may seem strange, but it was common practice for heads of monastic houses to be succeeded by relatives in that period, because ownership of land, on which the monasteries depended for their very existence, was not very secure.

We can see the beginnings of a parochial system in incidents connected with the Bishop's dedication of churches, for example that built by a thane called Puch, 'Not far from our monastery, about two miles distant', as it is described, and though unnamed identified with Bishop Burton. John was pressed to dine afterwards, and, as Puch's wife was very ill, he sent her holy water, used in the church's dedication, to drink, and she recovered. Again a dying man in what is generally agreed to be Cherry Burton was visited by John after another church consecration – a coffin for him was already in the room! After praying, the Bishop 'went out with the usual comforting words: "Hurry up and get well".' The man lived.

Contemporaries called these recoveries, which we might describe as happy coincidences, miracles, but, before modern medicine, many natural recoveries must have seemed like miracles. John obviously discouraged people from thinking that he had miraculous powers of healing, and his

Memorial tablet of St. John of Beverley in Beverley Minster. (Stephen Robinson)

sensible attitude is endearing. Saints usually have their feet very much on the ground.

The life-style of a seventh/eighth-century bishop is illustrated in the story of one of his young clergy, Herebald, later Abbot of Tynemouth, who was hurt in a fall from his horse while travelling in the Bishop's party. Young laymen in the group persuaded John, rather against his better judgment, to let them race their horses on a good road. He forbade Herebald to join in, but the young cleric had a fine horse, and eventually he could resist no longer, and raced off, took a bad fall, hitting his head on a stone. His disobedience shows that John was not too formidable a personality, while his distress at the accident was obvious. Herebald at first 'lay as though dead', and John spent all night praying for him. In the morning he came to Herebald. 'Can you live?' he asked. 'I can do so with the help of your prayers,' Herebald replied. The Bishop asked who had baptised him, and, when told the name of the priest said, '. . . you were not validly baptised, for I know him, . . . he was so slow witted that he could not learn how to instruct and baptise. For this reason, I ordered him to cease presuming to exercise his ministry –'. When he recovered, Herebald was re-baptised, 'cleansed in the lifegiving waters of Baptism'. There is much theological emphasis on the necessity for baptism to obtain salvation and eternal life in the early church, a factor which heightened missionary fervour in a pagan world.

The second great man with local connections was Willibrord, Archbishop of Utrecht, still alive when Bede finished writing his history, though longing 'with all his heart for the prize of a heavenly reward'. He was the son of a man called Wilgils, described as a householder, presumably a substantial farmer but not a noble, who became first a monk, and then a hermit somewhere on Spurn Point, 'on the headland surrounded by the ocean and the River Humber'. Here a small congregation gathered round him. Alcuin of York, the great English scholar of the eighth century, who spent half his life in charge of the famous school at York and half at Charlemagne's court, was a relative who eventually inherited the property of this little cell, and wrote a life of his kinsman. Willibrord was educated at Ripon, became a priest, and spent time in Ireland, like St. Chad and so many other English people who went there for religious studies, or to embrace the ascetic discipline of Irish monasticism, for the Irish, as Bede says, 'welcomed them all kindly, and without asking for any payment, provided them with books and instructors'. Did the best students go to Ireland for higher studies? The part played by Ireland in the early English Church make it appropriate that the first Bishop of Middlesbrough, Richard Lacy, was Irish, and so many of our priests have come from Ireland.

The English seem to have felt a responsibility to convert their pagan cousins on the Continent, their own blood and bone, for, after all, not many generations separated them. Egbert, an influential Englishman living in Ireland, who eventually persuaded the monks of Iona to conform to the Roman Easter, was prevented from travelling to the Continent himself as a missionary, but he despatched others to Frisia (Belgium and the Netherlands). First Wictbert, who was unsuccessful, and then, around 690, Willibrord, described by Bede as 'an outstanding priest of radiant virtue'.

Willibrord acted circumspectly, and made his way to Peppin, Duke of the Franks, whose support was crucial. Peppin had recently established his authority over the western parts of Friesland, and he now gave permission to Willibrord to preach. As in England, where the ruler was supportive, then missionary work could proceed; otherwise little could be achieved and indeed it could be dangerous to continue. Two English priests, the Hewards, were murdered at this time by the Saxons, and their bodies slung into the Rhine. Willibrord, intent on correctly establishing his ground work, then went off to Rome for Papal approval, and to collect relics with a view to substituting their veneration for that of idols, so showing a nice grasp of the way to win hearts and minds to the Faith.

There were other Englishmen working in the area, one of whom, Suidbert, was sent back to England by Peppin to be consecrated bishop by St. Wilfrid, our powerful Northumbrian bishop, during one of his freelance periods when exiled from Northumbria. However, when Suidbert retired to the monastery he established at Kaiserworth, Willibrord was sent to Rome by Peppin in 696 to be consecrated archbishop by Pope Sergius, with Utrecht as his see. The Pope gave him the name of Clement. He worked hard, preaching, converting, building churches and establishing monasteries, not confining his efforts to the parts of Frisia controlled by Peppin, but also bravely seeking out King Rathbod of Frisia. With him he was unsuccessful, for he 'could not soften his stony heart with the consolations of eternal life', as Alcuin says. Rebuffed, he then tried Denmark, 'the most savage peoples of the Danes', but their king was not interested, so he left, taking with him 30 Danish boys, baptising and instructing them in the hope that they might one day return as missionaries to their own people. Sheltering from a storm on this journey at Heliogoland, a pagan sanctuary, he ordered animals on the island to be slaughtered as food for his party and baptised three men in a spring, so violating pagan traditions. An outraged King Rathbod 'planned to avenge . . . the injuries to his own gods', and summoned Willibrord to him. The Bishop faced him fearlessly: 'For there is no God but one, who created heaven and earth . . . whoever worships him in true faith shall have everlasting life.' In reply the King said, 'I see that you have not feared our threats, and your words are just like your deeds.' He was doubtless in danger, but Rathbod, perhaps unwilling to antagonise Peppin, released him.

Bede says that in 731 Willibrord had been a bishop for 36 years, 'much revered for his great age', and had appointed suffragan bishops, 'choosing them from among the brethren who had come with him to preach'. Conditions in missionary territory meant appointments and consecrations were often made on 'the hoof', very different from today's church. Willibrord died in 738 and was buried in his monastery of Echternach in Luxembourg. The illuminated Echternach Gospels were probably made for him, and in the Bibliothèque Nationale in Paris is a Calendar in which he entered his consecration by Pope Sergius in his own handwriting, adding the words 'although unworthy'. In Hull, apart from the University Chaplaincy in Newland Park, which is dedicated to Willibrord, we do not seem to remember him. He is honoured, however, in the Netherlands as their apostle, and we should be very proud that a local man was of such importance in the early European Church.

Bibliography
Bede, *A History of the English Church and People* (Penguin Classics 1956 edition).
Whitelock, Dorothy (ed.), *English Historical Documents Vol.I AD 500-1042*, (extracts from Alcuin's *Life of Willibrord*) (1979).
Hunter Blair, P., *Northumbria in the Days of Bede* (1976).
Hunter Blair, P., *Anglo-Saxon England* (1977).

The Religious Orders in Medieval Hull

by
Rev. David Grant

When Edward I granted a charter to his '*Villa Regis super Hull*' in 1299 there were no religious houses within the boundaries of the town, but inextricably linked with its foundation was the Cistercian Abbey of Meaux near Wawne. That story is well known and so need not be repeated here. However, we should look at Meaux as the most important religious house of the area before considering the others.

The Cistercians began as a reform movement among a group of monks in Burgundy who wanted to return to a more rigorous following of the Rule of St. Benedict than was being followed by the communities to which they belonged. In 1098 Robert of Molesme, together with his companions, Alberic and Stephen Harding (an Englishman) and several others, began to build a new monastery at Citeaux (in Latin – *Cistercianum*, hence the name of the order). The early years were difficult but in 1112 the then Abbot Stephen Harding was approached by a young nobleman and a group of companions seeking to enter the abbey. The young nobleman was Bernard of Clairvaux, one the most important figures in the history of the Middle Ages.

When Bernard died in 1153 the Cistercians had 350 abbeys. It was an era of reform and renewal in the Church and the Cistercians were in the vanguard. The first house of the order in northern England was founded at Rievaulx in 1131. Fountains Abbey was founded in 1132 by monks disturbed by the laxity they perceived in their original home, St. Mary's Benedictine Abbey in York.

Meaux was founded from Fountains in 1151 by William le Gros, Count of Aumale (often anglicised as Earl of Albermarle) who had extensive land holdings in Yorkshire and Lincolnshire. William had already founded Thornton Abbey in 1139 for the Augustinian Canons and in 1147 Vaudey Abbey near Bourne for the Cistercians. While in Lincolnshire inspecting the progress of Vaudey, the Count met Adam, one of the original band of dissident monks from York who founded Fountains. William must have

The remains of Meaux Abbey

spoken to Adam about a vow he had made to go on a crusade to the Holy Land but was unable to fulfil because of his age and state of health. Adam received a dispensation from the Pope for William to found yet another monastery in commutation for his unfulfilled vow and so Meaux was founded. If that were not enough, Adam then chose a piece of land for the site of the new monastery which William had not long since bought from John de Melsa intending to turn it into a deer park. The Count tried to persuade Adam to take another part of his estates without success, and so one of the most powerful men in England had to bow to the wishes of a poor but stubborn monk!

The new abbey attracted further donations both from William and other benefactors and soon the abbey had holdings in Routh, Wawne, Keyingham, Sutton, Leven, Warter and Cottingham, not to mention places further afield. However, it seems that Abbot Adam, despite his gift of persuasion, was not a good manager and so the community was forced to disperse in 1160 and Adam retired to the Gilbertine monastery at Watton near Driffield for seven years. He was succeeded by Abbot Philip, who took a considerable gamble by taking on a sizable debt to Aaron, a Jewish moneylender (the house reputed to belong to Aaron can still be seen in Lincoln) in return for land at Wharram le Street. Aaron offered favourable terms but died in 1186 before the debt could be discharged. As the Jewish community had a special relationship with the Crown, the King took over as creditor and once more the Meaux community faced a major financial crisis as Richard I was not inclined to offer the same favourable terms as Aaron. This same king was to cause more problems because the community had to give up a year's income from its wool to help pay the ransom to free Richard from imprisonment in Austria in 1193.

The Meaux monks' main source of income was wool, their English name the 'white monks' was because their habits were made of undyed sheep's wool. The monks caused existing watercourses to be improved or else created new ones as the most practical way of getting wool and other produce to market. Eschedike linked the Abbey to the River Hull. Monkdike diverted part of the Lambwath stream into Eschedike. The Lambwath stream had its source near Aldbrough and formed a mere between Rise and Burton Constable. The hamlet of Marton was originally Mere-town. The Fordike also carried water from the Lambwath, as did Skernedike. It was only in 1973 that the lower reaches of the Fordike were filled in, rendered unnecessary by developments in modern drainage. In 1270 the Abbey owned about 11,000 sheep and Robert, the Abbot at that time, was able to negotiate with the merchants of Luca to supply them with 120 sacks. However, sheep scab and other problems took their toll. We know that in 1320 Meaux produced 25 sacks of wool; this compares with 76 at Fountains and 60 at Rievaulx.

Another important element in the medieval economy was fish. Church laws were strict about the number of fast days and seasons when abstinence from meat was total. Also fresh meat was hard to come by and so fish was an important element in the diet. The Cistercians were not allowed to eat meat at all except when ill or after being bled (a fairly common practice in medieval society thought to improve one's health) when recovering in the infirmary. A famous trial by combat was held to settle a dispute between Meaux and St. Mary's Abbey, York, over the fishing rights in Hornsea Mere. William the Conqueror had given Holderness to Odo, Count of Champagne, who was the third husband of his sister Adelaide. It was Odo, who had been present at the foundation of St. Mary's Abbey, who gave Hornsea to the York monks. In the 1250s Meaux claimed the right of fishing the mere and St. Mary's Abbey disputed their claim. The result was no fewer than two duels before the case was settled. The monks themselves did not fight but hired champions, who fought not to the death but until one side was judged to be the stronger. The 19th-century historian of Holderness, Poulson, drawing on the Meaux Chronicle describes what happened:

'William, the Abbot of Meaux, provided champions for the combat, the same number being found by the Abbot of St. Mary; a horse was first swum across the mere, and stakes were fixed to mark the extent of the boundary of the claim. On the day appointed for the combat, the parties and their champion appearing properly accoutred, the fight commenced and lasted, according to the narrator, from morning until the evening, when the champions of the plaintiff were beaten to the ground, and the fishery ultimately relinquished by the Abbot of Meaux.'

The Abbey's greatest crisis came in the next century. Bubonic plague was endemic at this period but by far the worst outbreak appeared in the middle of the 14th century. The Black Death, as it has been called, devastated much of Europe, and monastic communities, where most people lived in close proximity to their neighbours, were, perhaps, especially vulnerable. On 12 August 1349 the Abbot and five monks died; out of a community of 50 monks and lay brothers only ten were destined to survive.

The history of the Abbey was not merely a catalogue of problems. Between 1160 and 1253 the main buildings were completed, and, the High Altar was consecrated in 1253. We know that by 1269 the belfry had a great bell called '*Benedict*'; much later a second great bell, '*Jesus*', was added together with three smaller ones. The church rising out of the flat Holderness countryside must have been a magnificent sight. Its interior was decorated with glazed tiles made by craftsmen in kilns erected for the purpose a short distance from the buildings. Many of these have survived, thanks to the efforts of the late G. K. Beaulah. They are now in the care of English Heritage, though unfortunately not on permanent display.

The community had a strong connection with a priest thought by many people in Holderness to be a saint. In the early years of the 14th century Philip of Beverley held the living of Keyingham and was a noted scholar. A member of University College, Oxford, he was a doctor of theology and an expert on the philosophy of Aristotle, on which rested so much of scholastic theology. Philip ministered in Keyingham from 1311 to 1325, during which time, as well as his normal priestly duties, he was instrumental in building a chapel in Molescroft dedicated to Our Lady, and in those pre-seminary days he set up fellowships for clergy from Yorkshire to study at Oxford. Philip died in 1325 and his burial place in Keyingham church became associated with miracles which seemed to give a clear indication of his sanctity. The monks already owned land in Keyingham and eventually acquired the ownership of the church there and thus had a strong interest in the cult of this local saintly character.

We are fortunate in knowing so much about Meaux history through the survival of the chronicle of Thomas Burton who was Abbot 1396-99. A grave slab incised with the figure of an abbot, now preserved in Wawne church, is reputed to be his. Thomas became abbot at the time when the good government of the Church was seriously impeded by the Great Schism. Rival claimants to the papacy sought support wherever it could be found and strong-minded clerics resorted to drastic measures to ensure that their influence was upheld. Abbot Robert Burley of Fountains (1384-1410) was such a man and thought that, as Meaux was a daughter house of Fountains, he had the right to ensure that Thomas Burton, his candidate, was elected as abbot. He made his feelings very clear by deploying a company of archers outside Meaux gatehouse.

Burton represented the Yorkshire abbots at the Cistercians' general chapter in Vienna, which suggests he was held in high regard. While Burton was away, the meddlesome Abbot Burley decided as the head of Meaux's mother house to punish those who had opposed Burton's election. These monks appealed to Rome and Burton, rather than involve his monastery in protracted and expensive legislation, resigned his abbacy. It was during this period of voluntary exile at Fountains that he compiled the chronicle. He was blind for the last eight years of his life and died in 1437.

Records show that most of the Meaux community were local men and recruitment was constant, the number of new members that professed balancing the number of those who died. The majority of the community came from yeoman stock, the very class most involved in the Pilgrimage of Grace, that popular and conservative protest of late 1536 against the religious changes engineered by Henry VIII and his reviled Vicar General, Thomas Cromwell. Although several Cistercian abbots were involved in the protest, and locally included the Prior of the Augustinian house in Bridlington and the Sub-prior of the Gilbertine house at Watton, it appears only one Meaux monk, Bashlare, was involved. The protesters were persuaded to disperse as they made the fatal mistake of trusting the King. When the opportunity presented itself the Duke of Norfolk dealt with the ring leaders with such ruthless severity that any remaining resistance ebbed away.

The end came for Meaux in December 1539. Abbot Richard Stopes and 24 monks signed the document surrendering the house, which had an annual income of £298. Much of the stone was used by Henry VIII to build the castle and blockhouses erected in Hull in the face of a perceived threat from the Continent. Ironically these buildings were to become a prison for many Catholic recusants in the years to come.

As well as the Meaux community, the Augustinian Canons had interests in the town. Holy Trinity church, despite its size, was technically a chapel of ease to Hessle, which was owned and cared for by Guisborough Priory, while St. Mary's church, Lowgate, was in the possession of North Ferriby Priory. But it was the Carmelite friars who were the first religious order to make a foundation in the town. The beginnings of the order are wrapped in obscurity. The legend within the order was that they were the spiritual descendants of the Old Testament prophets, Elijah and Elisha. The 1st Book of Kings 18; 18-46, tells the story of how Elijah defeated the followers of the pagan god, Baal, on Mount Carmel. The disciples of these prophets had the collective names, 'Sons of the prophets', but they had died out long before the Middle Ages. By 1155 a certain St. Berthold had collected ten hermits who lived a religious life near the grotto of the prophet on Mount Carmel. In 1163 Rabbi Benjamin de Tudela reported that the Christians had built a chapel in honour of Elijah there. A rule of life based on the rule of St. Augustine was drawn up for the hermits by St. Albert de Vercelli, the Patriarch of Jerusalem. After 1210 the order made other foundations throughout the Latin (Crusader) kingdom of Jerusalem. Eventually the Saracens made the position of the hermits more and more dangerous and many emigrated to Europe. In 1247 a general chapter was held at Aylesford in Kent, and an Englishman, St. Simon Stock, was elected superior general. It was under his guidance that the purpose and organisation of the order was changed. Permission was granted to found houses in towns as well as lonely places and the order largely ceased to be eremitical.

The Carmelites were friars, not monks. Monks had as their main purpose the worship of God, primarily through the Mass and Divine Office, and other employment was incidental. Although a member of a religious order, a monk had the obligation of stability and so normally did not move around to other houses of his order unless exceptional circumstances arose. A friar saw the exercise of a ministry as an essential part of his vocation, and the liturgy was seen as a preparation for this end. Also, a friar joined an order, not a particular house, and consequently could be sent anywhere his superiors thought fit. The original friars were mendicants: they owned nothing themselves as individuals and neither did their order – even their houses were administered by trustees. The dress of the Carmelites changed several times until it was standardised as a brown habit worn under a white mantle-type cloak, hence 'Whitefriars'. The Hull historian, Tickell, states that shortly after founding his new town, King Edward – 'In order to draw down a blessing on himself and it, and out of gratitude to God for all the favours bestowed upon him' – together with Sir Robert Oughtred and Sir Richard de la Pole, founded a house for Carmelite friars in the town in

1290. However, the earliest mention of the house refers to 1289 when Robert of Scarborough, Dean of York, asked for permission to grant a messuage [a dwelling house with outbuildings and land] in Wyke upon Hull to the friars. The community was 13 strong when in 1298 the King gave 13 shillings for three days' food.

The original site proved to be too cramped and uncongenial and so in 1304 the King gave them a new site, three acres of land at Milncroft, outside the then boundaries of the town, from what is now Whitefriargate to Posterngate, and from Trinity House Lane to the town wall. This arrangement received formal papal approval from Clement V on 23 June 1307. The earliest surviving constitutions of the Carmelite order dating from 1324 show that the friars' lifestyle was very frugal: no meat was allowed and silence was greatly valued, while breaches of the rule were dealt with strictly. The Lancastrian kings (1399-1461) all chose their confessors from the Carmelites. The nobility saw the prayers of the friars, because they were mendicants, as being especially beneficial to their souls. In his will Sir Marmaduke Constable left a mark to all the houses of friars in York, Beverley and Hull in 1377, and Henry Lord Scrope left 20 shillings to the friars in Beverley and Hull. The merchant classes were generous, too, leaving both money and gifts in kind to the friars. In 1503 Beatrix Bellard wished to be buried in the Carmelites' church in Hull and wanted Masses to be celebrated for her soul as long as funds lasted; in other words she established a temporary chantry. Legacies were given for the celebration of 'trentals' (thirty Masses) by the friars and, according to the will of William Hapsham, it was customary for the friars to 'come and do dirige and mass according to the old custom of the town'. (*Dirige, Domine Deus meus* is the opening of Psalm 5 from the Office of the Dead). William left 6s. 8d. to each community of friars for this service and was buried in Holy Trinity church. In 1527 John Cokett also left 6s. 8d. to both communities on the condition that they attend his burial, eighth day mind [a traditional mass on the eighth day after burial] and anniversary. John was buried at the Charterhouse. The statue of Our Lady in the Carmelite church seems to have attracted considerable devotion. In 1486 Isabel Wilton gave an iron-bound chest and in 1501 Elizabeth Hatfield of Hedon gave two silver rosaries and a chalice. As late as 1523 Dame Joan Thurescrosse left £4 for the re-building of the church.

The end came on 10 March 1539 when Prior John Wade surrendered the friary to Richard Ingworth, himself a former friar, but by then a supporter of Henry VIII, who had been rewarded by being made Bishop of Dover. The King gave to Sir Thomas Heneage, a member of his court: 'All the house and site of the Whitefriary in Kingston upon Hull, and all houses, buildings, orchards and gardens thereunto belonging; also of 12d annual rent issuing out of the messuage called Trinity House'. By 1621 Alderman Thomas Ferres was the owner of the site and in that year under licence of James I gave it to Trinity House.

Some remains from the Carmelites' graveyard now rest in the crypt of the church of St. Charles in Jarratt Street. When the foundations of Smith's banking house (presently Poundstretcher) were being excavated in 1830 the remains were disturbed and subsequently removed to St. Charles with the permission of Fr. John Smith, the parish priest.

The second group of friars in Hull were officially called the hermits of St. Augustine but had as their usual name, Austin Friars. St. Augustine (died 430) lived a regular [*regula*: rule (Latin)] life with some of his clergy at Hippo, and a rule was drawn up embodying his principles. Various groups followed their own adaptations and this led to a considerable amount of confusion until the situation was reformed by Pope Alexander IV in 1256. Because of their black habit the Austins were often known as 'Blackfriars', especially in towns where the Dominicans, who were usually given that name, did not have a house. The Austins were probably brought to Hull by the de la Pole family. Although the family was not directly mentioned, but from a survey of the estates belonging to Sir William Sydney it is clear that the Sydneys claimed the rights of a founder. This was because in 1515 they had received part of the estates and privileges forfeited by Edmund de la Pole, the last Earl of Suffolk, which included those rights.

Simon of Pistoja, Prior General 1295-98, was in contact with William de la Pole the Elder, but there is no mention of the friars in Hull when Edward I gave alms to the friars in 1300. Their place is recorded in 1303 in the description of a neighbouring property held by Gilbert de Bedford. Another property, in the flesh market, bordered on their garden to the east, and a property owned by Thomas de la Pole was adjacent. Relatives of the Prior Provincial, Richard Wetwang, gave their help to the fledgling community. John Wetwang in 1317 gave a plot of land 204 x 115 feet for the construction of an oratory and house. Richard Wetwang, the rector of St. Deny's church in York, caused the east window of the church to be enlarged and the roof of the choir to be covered with lead. The gift of a large messuage by Sir Geoffrey de Hotham, also in 1317, proved to be a mixed blessing as it incurred a tax liability when Sir Geoffrey died. Although the Corporation of Hull was willing to donate its share of the tax money to the friars in return for their prayers, the Crown was not so generous. The matter dragged on until Sir Geoffrey's son, Richard, together with John of Wilflet, agreed to transfer the tax liability to other properties in their possession.

Church of the Augustinian Friary, Blackfriargate, 1789 (Kingston upon Hull City Council).

Like their neighbours the Carmelites, the Austin Friars attracted the patronage not only of the local nobility but also the people of the town. In his will of 1391 Adam Corey asked to be buried in their church, providing ten pounds of wax to supply the candles at his funeral. Adam left 12d to each chaplain who came to his funeral and nine marks to one of the community, William of Bridlington, and five marks to the other Austin friars. John Constable of Halsham in Holderness gave 20 shillings in 1407. The Constables obviously continued to favour the friars as in 1482 one of John's descendants gave five shillings, 'to do an obit for my soule in the quere'. Lady Joan Thurescross, who had been a friend to the Carmelites, also left 20 shillings to the Austins, 'to buy a vestment withall'. Robert Wilflit, a mariner (probably a descendant of John Wilflit) in 1520 endowed lights before the shrines of Our Lady and St. Catherine. Thomas Prestone, who desired to be buried in the north aisle of the church, left £33. 6s. 8d. in 1451 for all that was necessary to re-roof it. The church must have been substantial because as late as the 18th century a tower standing six stories high still survived. Recent excavations on the site in preparation for the building of the new magistrates' courts have shown that the structure of the church went through at least three re-modellings. The archaeological record shows that it was largely built of brick, with stone used for the most prominent architectural features, in fact, a style of building not unlike Holy Trinity church a short distance away or St. James's church in Sutton. The excavations have uncovered a large number of burials, 44 in oak coffins mostly made of imported Baltic timber. As only the better-off could afford coffins this gives a clear indication that the friars enjoyed the patronage of the successful merchants of the town. The Austin friary in Hull was probably one of the largest in their province, and hosted chapter meetings in 1369, 1435 and 1472. It still numbered 18 members at the beginning of the 16th century. Alexander Ingram was Prior when the house was surrendered to the King on 10 March 1539, the last Austin friary in England to be suppressed.

The third and latest religious house was established a short distance outside the walls of the town. It belonged to the Carthusian Order. St. Bruno (1030-1101) was born in Cologne but spent a large part of his early life in Rheims, where he was ordained priest, became a teacher and eventually chancellor of the diocese, and was very much involved in reform. Bruno had, however, long wished to return as far as possible to a lifestyle based on that followed by the earliest hermit monks in the Egyptian desert. Consequently he, together with six companions, having gained the support of the Bishop of Grenoble, settled in a lonely Alpine location known as Chartreuse. Each monk lived as a hermit in a small dwelling, only coming together with the others for the Divine Office in the church. It seems uncertain that St. Bruno intended to found an order as he never wrote a rule of life. However, as numbers grew it became obvious that one was necessary. Guigo, the fifth prior of Chartreuse, committed the customs of the mother house to paper at the request of the priors of the other charterhouses. These *Consuetudines* combined elements from the Rule of St. Benedict, St. Jerome's letters, The Life of the Fathers, the writings of St. John Cassian and other influences.

Guigo's statutes were approved by Pope Innocent II in 1133 and formed the basis of all subsequent Carthusian legislation. In England Carthusian monasteries were known as 'Charterhouses' – probably a linguistic corruption of Chartreuse. By the end of the Middle Ages nine charterhouses had been founded in this country. The first was founded at Witham in Somerset in 1178 by Henry II as part of his penance for his involvement in the murder of St. Thomas of Canterbury. Hugh, the first prior, was sent from Chartreuse to Witham, from where in 1186 he went to Lincoln as its bishop. As St. Hugh of Lincoln his shrine was venerated in the cathedral there until the Reformation.

The foundation of the Charterhouse close to Hull only resulted when plans to establish other forms of community life came to nothing. The

Hull historian, Tickell, states that a college of six priests was established on the site by Edward I. Sir William de la Pole, the first Mayor of Hull, knighted by Edward III in 1337, acquired the patronage of this community together with other lands in the Myton lordship. These secular priests appear to have been unsatisfactory and were replaced by Franciscans, but they in turn did not last long. Sir William then decided to pull down the original buildings and replace them with a hospital for a number of chaplains and poor people. This project received a licence from the King but then the plan was changed yet again, this time in favour of 13 Minoresses (Poor Clare nuns) and a number of poor people. Further royal permission was given to transfer the advowson (the right of presentation to a benefice) of Frisby, North Cave and Foston to the nuns. Perhaps the previous religious foundations had not been economically viable and so Sir William decided upon a less ambitious project, namely a house for nuns, but this time properly funded. Whatever he intended, he was not to see it through as he died on 21 June 1366.

Eventually Sir William's son, Michael, who was to become Earl of Suffolk and Lord Chancellor, changed the plan yet again in 1377-78, this time in favour of the Carthusians. In the foundation charter of February 1378 Michael declared his affection and respect for the Carthusian order and his belief that they would serve God better than the nuns. Other nobles connected with the new foundation were Richard Scrope of Bolton in Wensleydale, who was married to Michael's sister, Blanche, together with Walter Fauconberg, Richard Ferriby and Robert Selby. In 1384 Michael established a hospital for 13 poor men and 13 poor women which came to be known as the 'Hospital of St. Michael, commonly called God's house without the gates of Hull'. The master was always to be a secular priest, not a monk, and the first one was Robert de Killum. The monks and the inmates of the hospital did not live under the same roof although the buildings were close to each other and it would seem that the Prior had some say in the management of the hospital. Despite this promising start, Michael's impeachment for treason and his death in Paris in 1386 meant that the monks were not able to benefit in full from his endowments. His son, Michael, the second Earl, restored the family to royal favour and in 1397 gave lands and goods which brought in £2. 18s. 4d. per year. In 1402 Richard, Lord Scrope, and Edmund de la Pole (brother of the first Earl) gave lands worth £20 per year. In 1404 Marmaduke Constable of Flamborough left the monks £20. Earl Michael in 1408 gave lands and rents in Hessle, West Ella, Myton, Willerby, Tranby and North Ferriby. John Dautre left the monks a silver plate inscribed 'Jesu' in 1437. A chalice and 100 shillings were left to the community by Sir Thomas Cumberworth in 1450. It is interesting to note, bearing in mind the Carthusians' rejection of worldly pomp and show and anonymity in death, that Michael de la Pole and John, Lord Neville, of Latimer, requested blank burial stones. This was in sharp contrast to some of the funerals in Holy Trinity church at the same period where testators left detailed instructions about how many pounds of wax should be bought for the candles and torches which were to be burnt on the day of their funeral. Even elaborately embroidered bedspreads were used to add yet more display: in 1490 Thomas Wood, a Hull draper, left instructions that his best bed should go over his grave each year at his *Dirige* and *Requiem*, and should be hung up in Holy Trinity church on St. George's Day, 'emong other worshipfull beddes'. Several of the de la Poles were buried in the monks' church, Sir William and his wife before the High Altar and Michael and his wife in the chancel. William, fourth Earl and first Duke, who was murdered at sea in 1450, was first buried at Wingfield in Suffolk but his remains were later moved to the Charterhouse. Alice, William's widow, chose to be buried at Ewelme in Oxfordshire, where William had re-built the church, but she did not forget the Charterhouse in her will. She also stipulated that the Prior was to have statues erected of her and William each holding a jug in one hand and a dish in the other. The Prior was then to distribute food and drink to two of the inmates of the hospital every day in front of these statues. If this instruction was neglected the monks were to forfeit £10.

This was not the first time that a gift came along with a penalty clause. John Colthorpe, who had been Mayor of Hull in 1389, and his wife, Alice, endowed a dwelling in the cloister for a monk who would offer Mass daily for their souls and those of all the faithful departed. When the monk who occupied the house died, the Prior and community were to replace him within three months or else be fined £40 payable to the Mayor and Corporation.

Relations with the authorities of the town were not always cordial. In 1454 the Mayor, Richard Anson, went to London to complain to the Privy Council about the encroachments of the Prior on property held by the town. As we have seen, the de la Pole family always took a great interest in the Charterhouse and, when resident in Hull at the Suffolk Palace, would frequently visit to attend Mass and other services in the church. In 1465 the Duke's steward applied to the Corporation for permission to have a postern gate cut in the town wall opposite the Charterhouse to enable the Duke, together with his wife and mother, to get there without having to pass through the streets. Permission was granted as it would have been difficult to refuse the request of such a powerful family, but it was made clear that it was not to create a precedent.

Community life, even that of the Carthusians, sometimes caused tensions, especially when there was a grievance either real or imagined. The Calendar of entries in the Papal Registers records the name of William Cuerton, a monk who left the Hull Charterhouse without permission and still wearing his habit, and who went to the Curia in Rome because he considered that he was being 'persecuted'. In 1477 he was absolved from leaving his monastery without permission and allowed either to return or transfer to another; did he ever settle down?

When Henry VIII resolved to break with the Papacy and take the English Church into schism the most consistent opposition came from within the Carthusian order. The Prior of the London Charterhouse, John Houghton, together with Robert Lawrence, Prior of Beauvale and Augustine Webster, Prior of Axholme, refused to consent to the Act of Supremacy and were hanged, drawn and quartered at Tyburn on 4 May

1535. St. Thomas More saw them, going from the Tower to the place of execution and said to his daughter: 'Lo, dost thou not see, Meg, that these blessed fathers be now as cheerfully going to their deaths as a bridegroom to his marriage?' Three more members of the London community were executed in June, but more of them were still determined to resist. The King was faced with a difficulty, and the execution of such obviously good men as the Carthusians and Thomas More and John Fisher was regarded as a scandal both at home and abroad. The next ploy was to send some of the resolute monks to monasteries

Silver Madonna and Child – fragment from a reliquary or shrine, first half of the 15th century, found during the excavations of the town wall, Humber Street, 1964.
(Kingston upon Hull City Council).

23

which had conformed to the King's supremacy over the Church. Thus it was that John Rochester and James Walworth were sent from London to Hull in May 1536 on the anniversary of the martyrdom of the three priors. In the February of that year Archbishop Lee of York had persuaded the Priors of Hull and Mount Grace to come to a reluctant acceptance of the royal supremacy, although by the early summer the Hull monks were seen as being notable because they were conformable.

As a 'lesser house' with revenues of only £175 per year, the Hull Charterhouse should have gone in the first phase of dissolution: the Suppression Act of 1536 was aimed at houses with an income less than £200 but Sir Ralph Ellerker, Marmaduke Constable and other worthies petitioned Thomas Cromwell, the King's Vicar General, to keep the Charterhouse open: 'the prior and brethren are right well favoured and commended by the honest men of Hull and other neighbours thereabouts for their good living and great hospitality by them daily kept'. According to one account the Charterhouse had been suppressed in February and, when the monks returned, they found it stripped to the bare walls. Whatever happened, it must have been clear that the inevitable had merely been postponed. All but the most fervent must have been demoralised. Rochester and Walworth were still not broken.

The Pilgrimage of Grace [cf. Meaux above] began in autumn 1536, and in the early part of 1537 the insurgents tried to take Hull, but the Carthusians were not implicated. Maurice Chauncy, who had been with them in the London Charterhouse, wrote that a certain nobleman living in the neighbourhood reminded Cromwell about Rochester and Walworth and that they had not yet conformed. They were arrested and sent to York. On 22 March John Rochester wrote to the Duke of Norfolk, then acting as the King's vice-regent in the North. In the letter, which still exists, he sought an audience with Henry VIII to show him that the Act of Supremacy over the Church was directly against the laws of God, the Catholic Faith and the health of the King's body and soul. The simple plain speaking faith of a selfless holy man was completely alien to a self-centred pragmatist like Norfolk. Rochester's letter was sent to Cromwell together with a covering letter from the Duke in which he stated his opinion that the monk was one of the most arrogant traitors he had ever heard of and that he should be *'justified'*. John Rochester and James Walworth never went back to Hull. They were hanged in chains at York on 11 May 1537. They were declared 'Blessed' by Pope Leo XIII in 1886.

The Hull Charterhouse was finally suppressed on 9 November 1539. The last Prior, Ralph Mauleverer, was given a pension of 50 marks and the six other monks received £6. 13s. 4d. each. Some of the monks tried to continue their Carthusian vocation. Thomas Synderton joined the Charterhouse at Sheen in Queen Mary's reign. When Queen Elizabeth came to the throne he had to move yet again, this time to the Charterhouse at Bruges where he died in 1580. William Remington died in the Charterhouse at Perth in 1560. John Bennett, a monk connected with Hull, died at the Roermond Charterhouse in 1580.

The Charterhouse hospital did not fall with the monastery and still provides a home for elderly people, just as the de la Poles had intended. However, the earliest building now on the site only dates back to the 18th century.

What remains today of Hull's monastic past? Sadly, very little apart from some street names and the documentary and archaeological record, though several books which once belonged to Meaux Abbey and the Hull Charterhouse still survive. St. Benedict in his rule urges those who follow the consecrated life to 'Prefer nothing to the love of Christ'. The religious orders in medieval Hull tried to observe that precept. Today there are men and women in our city living in contemporary religious communities who are committed to that same ideal – they remind us that it is not an historical curio but a living reality.

Bibliography

Allison, K. J. (ed.), *History of the County of York, East Riding Vol. I The City of Hull* (Victoria County History, 1969).

Bradley, Edith, *The Story of the English Abbeys. Vol I, The Northern Counties* (1938).

Burton, Janet, *The Religious Orders in the East Riding of Yorkshire in the Twelfth Century* (East Yorkshire Local History Society, Beverley, 1989).

Calvert, Hugh, *A History of Kingston upon Hull* (1978).

Cross, Clair, *The End of Medieval Monasticism in the East Riding of Yorkshire* (East Yorkshire Local History Society, Beverley, 1993).

Duffy, Eamon, *The Stripping of the Altars* (Yale, 1992).

English, Barbara, *The Lords of Holderness* (Oxford ,1979).

Gillett, E. and MacMahon, K. A. *History of Hull* (Oxford, 1980).

Heath, Peter, 'The Evidence of Hull Wills', *The Church, Politics and Patronage, Urban Piety in the Fifteenth Century* (Gloucester, 1984).

Horrox, Rosemary, *The De la Poles of Hull* (East Yorkshire Local History Society, Beverley, 1983).

Hughes, Jonathan, *Pastors and Visionaries: Religion and Secular Life in late Medieval Yorkshire* (Woodbridge, 1988).

Knowles, David, *The Religious Orders in England* (Cambridge, 1959).

Logan, F. Donald, *Runaway Religious in Medieval England 1240-1540* (Cambridge, 1996).

Roth, Francis, *The English Austin Friars* (New York, 1966).

Wildridge, T. Tindall, *The White Friars, Black Friars and Carthusians of Kingston upon Hull* (Malet Lambert Local History Reprints, Hull, 1981).

Whatmore, L. E., *The Carthusians under King Henry the Eighth*. Analecta Cartusiana (Salzburg, 1983).

Medieval Archaeology Vol. XLI. 1997.

The Pilgrimage of Grace and Hull

by
Professor Barbara English

As the sixteenth century began, a variety of religious opinions, which would later be called Protestantism, gathered strength in Northern Europe. Ultimately such views would fissure the almost universal Catholicism of the European Middle Ages. It seems that these new ideas travelled across the North Sea from Europe, were especially current among seamen and flourished in seaports such as Hull.

In the 1530s the people of Hull, as a result of these influences, were probably less Catholic than their contemporaries in Beverley and the East Riding. The behaviour of Hull in 1536-1537 suggests an attachment to the King, and to his new ecclesiastical policies, which outweighed loyalty to the old religion: for these few months events at Hull dominated England and particularly the future of its church.

In the autumn of 1536 William Stapleton, a young lawyer on vacation from the Inns of Court, was ending his visit to the Greyfriars in Beverley, in company with his invalid brother, Christopher, and Christopher's wife. William Stapleton (whose home was Wighill in the West Riding) became one of the leaders of the Pilgrimage of Grace, the most serious of the rebellions against Henry VIII, which provided, perhaps, the last chance that England would remain a Catholic nation. Although Stapleton was not the prime mover in the rebellion, he was the captain who besieged and took Hull: so it is appropriate that his name should open the history of the Pilgrimage of Grace and Hull.

On Wednesday, 4 October 1536, the Stapletons said good-bye at 10.00 p.m., as William intended to cross the Humber from Hull with the tide at 7.00 a.m. But at 3.00 in the morning a servant woke him with the news that all Lincolnshire was in rebellion, from Barton to Lincoln. This first phase of the rebellion had begun in Louth parish church, after evensong on Sunday, 1 October. William Stapleton, during the next few days and weeks, found himself drawn deep into rebellion against the King.

The Pilgrimage of Grace (a name used to cover the rebellions of 1536-

1537 over a wide geographical area) is the first popular movement to provide historians with a rich source of primary material, from all sorts of men from lords to shoemakers. After the Pilgrimage, the leaders made lengthy confessions which the government recorded in a series of books and papers, later published as *The Letters and Papers of Henry VIII*. They make very good reading, including all sorts of details about the rebellion (such as the days and times in the paragraph above), and form the basis of all modern writing about the Pilgrimage. The King was very anxious to know the motives of the rebels, and some of the confessions are annotated in the margins by the King himself. Superficially, we seem to know everything about the rebellion. But the confessions may not be as revealing as they seem: some evidence was obtained under torture, when men may say what they think will please their torturers: most guessed they were going to be executed, so were driven either to implicate their fellows, or to save them (particularly to save their families), depending on their nature. In a later section, the pilgrims' motives will be considered: at present, we can return to William Stapleton in Beverley.

Nothing but rumour came to Stapleton until Sunday 8 October, when servants brought the news that the common bell of Beverley had been rung and that a proclamation had been made in the Market Place for everyone to take an oath, and to assemble first at the Hall Garth (the archbishop's manor house south of the Minster), and subsequently on Westwood Green, just outside the Greyfriars (the Franciscan house of friars, which lay between Westwood Road and the present Greyfriars Crescent). The Stapleton men were, they said later, trying to keep their family and servants safe within the Greyfriars, but on Sunday evening Lady Stapleton (she is unnamed) showed where her own inclinations lay:

> The wife of the said Christopher [Stapleton] went forth and stood in a close, where a great number of them [the Beverley rebels] were come of the other side of the hedge, and she saying 'God's blessing on you' and 'speed you well in your good purpose', they said 'where is your husband and his folks that he cometh not as others do?' And she said 'they be in the friars', go pull them out by the heads'.

Christopher, who evidently had difficulty in managing his wife, was very upset by this:

> wishing himself out of the world, saying unto her 'what do you mean except you would have me, my son and heir, and my brother cast away, and my heirs forever dis[in]herit[ed]?'.

She replied, in a significant phrase: 'It was God's quarrel.'

William Stapleton now decided, he said in his confession, to join the rebels in order to moderate their behaviour, and he was soon joined by his brother's son, Brian. On Monday night some men went to raise Cottingham and Hessle, and some went to fire Hunsley beacon, to raise the adjoining villages. The beacon lay on the ground, so they 'made great fires of hedges and haystacks' instead: on Wednesday night both Hunsley and Tranby beacons were lit. On Thursday the rebels at Beverley learned that 'all Holderness' had risen, and some prisoners had been taken; other men of standing, including Sir John Constable (of Halsham and Burton Constable), Sir John his son, Sir William Constable, Sir Ralph Ellerker, Edward Roos, Walter Clifton, Philip Miffin and John Hedge of Bilton, had all fled to Hull. These escapees from the rebels make an interesting list, for the Constables and the Ellerkers were, in subsequent decades, to remain staunchly Catholic and suffer heavy penalties accordingly. But in 1536 they seem to have felt their loyalty to the King overruled their religious preferences. The Stapletons sent messengers to Hull 'to the Mayor, Aldermen and commons, to know whether they would do as we did, or be against us': the answer to be brought to Weighton hill.

On Friday, 13 October (the day the Lincolnshire Rising collapsed, although that news had not reached Yorkshire), four envoys came from Hull to the assembly at Weighton: Browne and Harrison, former sheriffs, and the merchants, Kemsey and Saull. These offered to give up the town of Hull, perhaps in fear of the looting that had taken place in Lincolnshire when the rebels had been opposed. The envoys and the Stapletons went to talk to Robert Aske, who was also at Weighton – Aske, of Aughton, was the chief Captain and had already raised Howdenshire and Marshland. Aske decided to go on to take York, and sent William Stapleton and his men to take Hull. It was on his march to York that Aske began to talk of the rising as a pilgrimage, telling his messengers that they were pilgrims. At York he drew up the pilgrim's oath, which began:

> Ye shall not enter into this our Pilgrimage of Grace for the commonwealth, but only for the love that ye do bear unto Almighty God, his faith, and the Holy Church . . . to the preservation of the King's person and his issue, to the purifying of the nobility and to expulse all villein blood and evil councillors.

At Hull, William Stapleton, with Nicholas Rudston and George Metham (whose family were early recusants), went into 'the church' (presumably Holy Trinity) to meet the gentry who had fled from Holderness, and tried to persuade them to join. Sir John Constable the elder stated his determination to die rather than join, saying 'he would rather die with honesty than live with shame'. The debate was followed by breakfast, and then a further meeting in the church, where the Mayor, in the presence of the Aldermen and gentlemen, said 'they would keep their town as the King's town'; if any wished to join the rebels they might do so, but the town would given them no aid, no 'horse nor harness, meat nor money'.

Stapleton and his fellows rode back to Weighton with this gloomy news: he was, as he said, becoming very exhausted by the continual to-and-fro journeys. He then went to Bishop Burton to negotiate with Sir Christopher Hildyard and other gentlemen who had come to Beverley with the men of Holderness: and that night the leaders planned the siege of Hull, arranging to meet at 9 o'clock in the morning of Sunday, 15 October, at a tree called Windy Oak in Cottingham. While the men of Yorkswold went back to Aske and towards York, the other troops were stationed around Hull in this way: two hundred Holderness men on the east of the River Hull, and the Beverley men at Sculcoates on the west bank; next was Thomas Ellerker with the men of Cottingham, and at Hull hermitage on Humber bank a further hundred Holderness men and those from Hullshire.

The siege of Hull continued for five days. During that time Stapleton claimed he struggled to maintain order. Men of the Beverley Water Towns (Woodmansey, Tickton, Weel and Hull Bridge), old enemies of Hull, offered to burn all the ships lying in the haven at Hull and the town beside, by sending down-river burning barrels of pitch: a very effective weapon against wooden shipping. Stapleton prevented this: he also saved the windmills at the Beverley Gate of Hull, but was less successful in saving oxen, a crane, a peacock, some pigs, a quantity of hay and a pet lamb of the Mayor's. There was, inevitably, some petty crime: a thieving butcher who had been put in charge of the food, and a Beverley sanctuary man, a pickpocket, were seized, and as a punishment the pickpocket was keelhauled. He survived and both were expelled from the force.

Negotiations between the besieged and the besiegers continued, with meetings at Hull Charterhouse. One negotiator for Stapleton was John Wright of Holderness: it is a common name, but perhaps he was one of the Wrights of Plowland, a recusant family which was to provide two members of the Gunpowder Plot conspiracy. The Hull garrison was inclined to surrender, although their resistance was stiffened by Sir John Constable. Finally, on the approach of a further force of rebels, the town and the gentry yielded, sending Aldermen Elland and Knowles to Stapleton, and opening the town gates. The sole condition of the surrender was that no-one would be forced to take the Pilgrims' oath. It was Friday, 20 October 1536. The siege of Hull was over: Sir Robert Constable of Flamborough

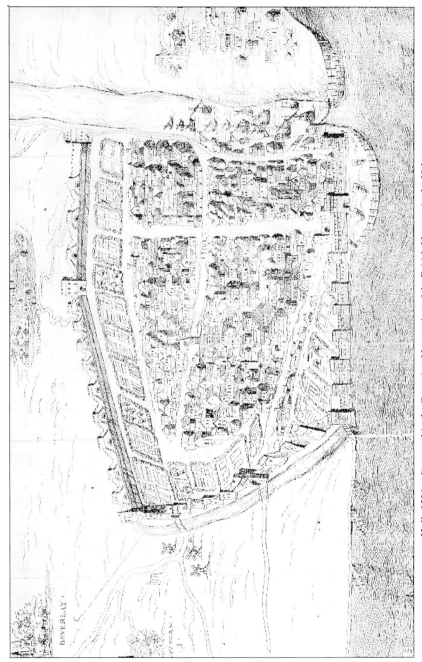

Hull c1530 – discovered in the Cottonian Manuscripts of the British Museum in the 19th century.
(Kingston upon Hull City Council).

and Holme on Spalding Moor took command of the town, with a garrison of two hundred men. Constable strengthened the defences and requisitioned ships and customs dues for the rebels: against the will of the town, according to their later statement. Hull was held for the pilgrims in this way until the end of the rising, early in December, when peace was made at Doncaster, and in the presence of the King's general, the Duke of Norfolk, Aske knelt down and gave up his title of Great Captain. The pilgrims took off the badges of the Five Wounds of Christ and went home.

One of the men who had joined William Stapleton at Beverley in 1536 was John Hallam, a farmer from Cawkeld near Driffield. He combined with Sir Francis Bigod of Settrington to raise a further rebellion in January 1537: an epilogue to the main revolt, but one that allowed the King to take vengeance on the North for their alleged breach of the terms of peace.

Bigod and Hallam's revolt came from the distrust that remained, on both sides, after the Doncaster agreement. The King was, by all accounts, angry with the terms Norfolk had made – a pardon for all, a Parliament at York, a restoration of the monasteries. Would the King honour this agreement? For his part, the King must have wondered if the North would rise again? Through the rest of December the rumours of the King's intentions ran around the north country. Why was the King planning to fortify Hull and Scarborough, unless it was to suppress eastern Yorkshire?

Sir Francis Bigod was an impoverished aristocrat from an ancient family, while his ally, John Hallam, represented the yeomen, the ordinary farmers, the common people of the Fast Riding. All through the Pilgrimage there had been an uneasy alliance between gentry and commoners. Both sides distrusted each other, and historians dispute their respective degrees of responsibility. Were the gentry manipulating rebellion from the wings, or were they coerced into leadership by the commons, as they subsequently claimed? Bigod and Hallam, beside being of different classes, had different religious views. Hallam was a religious conservative, wanting the maintenance of the old Catholic church. Bigod, though, had reforming ideas. He wanted parish churches to be taken back from the minsters and monasteries that owned them, in order to strengthen the position of the parish priests. He was also an ardent supporter of the idea that the King and not the Pope should be the head of the Church in England. All his recorded views in the early 1530s were 'Protestant' ones, which makes it surprising indeed that he joined the Pilgrimage of Grace, which he did, he claimed reluctantly, at York. His motives in 1537 appear to have been fear of the King's revenge, even though Aske and others assured him his fears were groundless.

Sir Francis Bigod was brought up in the household of Cardinal Wolsey, where he became friendly with another member of the household, Thomas Cromwell, who was to manage the Protestant reformation for the King. Bigod remained on good terms with Cromwell, and all his surviving letters, including the last on the eve of his execution, were written to Cromwell. He went to Oxford, probably to Wolsey's 'Cardinal College' (later Christ Church), and it may have been there that he first came into contact with Protestant ideas. Hallam, on the other hand, was a poor man from a lonely farm about a mile from Watton priory. He was described by his confederates as 'so cruel and fierce a man amongst his neighbours that no man durst disobey him'.

The Christmas holiday of 1536-1537 was a long holiday, taking in the Twelve Days of Christmas and then Plough Monday, 8 January: days when men met each other, with time for talking, the gentry meeting in their houses, and the commoners in the ale houses, and both at and around the churches and the abbeys. It was a particularly cold Christmas, and, in the south, the King's court went down to the feast at Greenwich over the frozen Thames. Almost all the conspiracy between Bigod and Hallam was planned in this Christmas time, mainly in and around Watton, and particularly at the Gilbertine priory there. Hallam made his headquarters at Watton parish church and John Bell's ale house. On 8 January, after drinking at John Bell's, the villagers held a meeting at Watton guildhouse to count the 'plough money' for the church. The meeting over, four of the men turned into the church to say a Pater Noster, and there, by Our Lady's altar, Hallam expressed his fears that the gentlemen would betray the commons once Hull and Scarborough were fortified.

Two days later (Wednesday, 10 January 1537) Bigod with four servants arrived at Hallam's house at Cawkeld. They walked to Watton priory together, and dined there with the subprior and at least two of the brethren (the recently appointed prior, Robert Holgate, turncoat and future archbishop of York, had fled to the south). At Watton after dinner Bigod and Hall left the canons by the fire, and withdrew into the window (the oriel window in the prior's lodging at Watton still remains) where they discussed the King's pardon, and its dangerous ambiguities. The plot to rekindle the rising was outlined at Watton, and refined some days later at Bigod's house at Settrington.

Bigod and Hall planned to take both Hull and Scarborough at the same time, and hold them until Parliament should meet: Bigod was to take Scarborough, Hallam Hull. They expected simultaneous risings in Richmondshire and Durham. A. G. Dickens, who has written the only modern account of Bigod and Hallam's rising, sees this plan, though abortive, as 'the most interesting politico-military concept evolved by a

Tudor rebel'. The plan showed the possibilities of holding towns as bargaining counters, and also the crucial importance of Hull in a Yorkshire rebellion – to be demonstrated by Hull's role in the Civil War a century later. It was strategically a great advance on the aimless marchings of the 1536 rebellion, for Aske had taken no steps to take a pledge to ensure the King kept his bargain – with hindsight, Aske could have kept York.

Hallam set out from Watton in the dark of the morning of Tuesday, 16 January, to take Hull, accompanied by about twenty men: thirteen of them are identified in the records, the clerk of Beswick, Kitchen, a glover from Beverley, a man from Newbald and nine men from Watton, one described as a yeoman and the rest either labourers or servants of the priory. What real chance did they have? Pretending to have something to sell, they entered Hull two or three at a time, sheltering with the crowds that were coming into the town on this, a market day. Hallam rode in wearing 'a privy coat of fence made with many folds of linen cloth rosined, and a privy skull on his head'. Perhaps his men might have had leather waistcoats and daggers – maybe swords. The plan was that Hallam would go to the Market Place, and then shout, 'Come hither to me all good commoners', when the small band would take the town. But as they went through the gate into Hull, they had already been betrayed by one of their number, Fowberry of Newbald.

Hallam had expected the Hull people to be ready to rise: why, it is not clear. He also expected reinforcements from Holderness, but they had not come. Seeing the hopelessness of his band taking Hull, he rode out of the town, halting at the watering place beside the windmills outside the town walls. As he turned back to look at Hull, he saw the town gates being closed. The clerk of Beswick said to him, 'Will you go your ways and leave your men behind you?' Hallam, with more honour than sense, turned back in a vain attempt to extricate his men, and, after a long sword-fight at the gate, was arrested by Elland and Knowles, the same two Aldermen who had surrendered the town in 1536.

Meanwhile Bigod had been no more successful at Scarborough. Bigod decided to join in the attack on Hull, as the more important town. But he was too late: delaying to collect men at the mustering point at Bainton, he heard that Hallam had failed, and a cluster of messages told him that those he had hoped would be his allies, such men as Aske, Robert Constable and Ellerker, who had been 'out' in 1536, were proclaiming their belief in the King's peace. The Ellerkers led an attack on Bigod in Beverley on Friday, 19 January, and captured most of his men: he fled first towards Settrington and then to Sandsend, the little village on the coast below his castle of Mulgrave, where he hid while the castle was emptied of its goods by the

King's officers. He was finally caught in a chapel in Cumberland in March. He was executed at Tyburn: Hallam was executed at Hull. Many of the rebels of 1536 now also suffered the extreme penalty as Henry VIII took his revenge, including Robert Aske, hanged in chains at York Castle, and the sub-prior of Watton, hanged in chains at his priory. Robert Constable, who had held Hull in 1536, was hanged there 'on Friday, being market day at Hull, above the highest gate of the town, so trimmed in chains . . . that I think his bones will hang there this hundred year' (and his remains were still there when Henry VIII visited the town in 1541). William Stapleton, however, was pardoned and lived until 1544.

There is an ongoing debate among historians about the reasons for the rebellions of 1536-1537. The evidence is so rich that there is sufficient material to support almost any interpretation. Political historians may see the Pilgrimage as one faction, one power group, against another, or as a class struggle of the gentry versus the state, or peasants versus their masters. One diplomatic historian believed it was a plot hatched in Vienna by friends of Catherine of Aragon, Henry's divorced queen. Economic historians write of high taxes, bad harvests, fear of unemployment with the closure of monasteries, the drain of northern money to the south. A case can be made for all these: and, in addition, almost all the pilgrims' complaints mentioned their dislike of religious changes. The complications of Henry VIII's divorce had led to the Act of Supremacy, by which Henry had made himself, instead of the Pope, head of the Church in England. While, in retrospect, this may have been the decisive moment in the break with Rome, it was barely mentioned in the rebels' grievances, and, apart from John Fisher and Thomas More, few people seemed to have understood the deep significance of the change. The divorce led to the fall of Cardinal Wolsey, replaced as chief minister by Thomas Cromwell, who had pushed forward the valuation of all church property in England (the *Valor Ecclesiasticus* of 1535, for which Sir Francis Bigod was one of the Yorkshire commissioners) and also closed some smaller monasteries (in East Yorkshire, Haltemprice and North Ferriby). These attacks on church property seemed to cause more resentment in 1536 than the more abstract matters of doctrinal change.

Wild rumours were current in the East Riding of 1536: in the words of William Stapleton: 'there was a common brute [rumour] in Yorkshire that diverse parish churches in that country should be put down and the goods therefore to be taken to the King's use'; this rumour was accompanied by one that church chalices of silver were to be replaced by brass. Religious houses were to be suppressed, and certain holidays abolished (Hallam protested when the parish priest of Watton announced that St. Wilfrid's day had been abolished by the King together with other holydays). This combined with the new religious opinions, and economic problems, which Stapleton also mentioned, 'did move, grudge and steer the people much to such rebellion'. Aske, the Great Captain, certainly believed that there was a threat to the old forms of religion, and he made a famous declaration in favour of the monasteries. Whatever other motives they may have had, the rebels joined in a Pilgrimage, a word chosen for its religious associations, under a banner and wearing the badge of the Five Wounds of Christ.

What was the position of Hull in 1536? The town seems, from the narrative given above, to have been unenthusiastic about the Pilgrimage, and to have been strongly opposed to Hallam and Bigod's revolt. Hull appears to have been more 'Protestant' than the surrounding countryside, although this name was not yet the label it was to become. The historian A. G. Dickens believed that Hull in the early 16th century contained more Protestantism than, say, York, perhaps through the influences coming into the port from Northern Europe; the Archdeacon of the East Riding reported in 1535 that all men in Hull were 'well inclined' towards the King's new title of Supreme Head. It is interesting that the Mayor in 1536 stated his wish 'to keep the town as the King's town'. This loyal stance was, however, quickly changed when the sack of the town was threatened, and the town surrendered, without a shot being fired.

My view of the position of Hull in 1536-1537 was that it was inclined to support the King, for religious and political reasons, and wished to stay out of the rebellion. But threatened with economic sanctions, the town was prepared to negotiate with the besiegers, dreading the burning of the town above all else. The position of the gentry who had taken refuge within the town strengthened the town's royalist inclinations: although, paradoxically, the same gentry families who in 1536 supported the King rather than the pilgrims were during the next two centuries to suffer for their support of the old religion, and Hull during the 17th century was to suffer for its opposition to the King.

After the rebellion was over, the Mayor, Aldermen and inhabitants of Hull received a letter of thanks from the King for their services: not for them the humiliation of the former Yorkshire rebels (including the Archbishop of York) who were forced, kneeling, to confess their faults to the King as he progressed through the county in 1541. Henry VIII had come to recognize the military significance of the town and port of Hull, and took a personal interest in strengthening the defences. The two Aldermen (Elland and Knowles) who had delivered the town to Stapleton in 1536, but who had later captured Hallam, were knighted in 1537, and in 1541 Henry himself twice visited Hull, granting privileges for the merchants and mariners. He arranged that Elland should be made Mayor, and that Elland and Knowles should oversee the building of new fortifications, which included improvement of the old de la Pole manor house.

Hull's reward for remaining (however ambiguously) on the royal side during the 1536-7 rebellions was to be advanced in royal favour. The extended fortifications brought new money into the town: the port became richer as the importance of sea trade and sea power increased. During the mid-16th century the town moved more decisively towards Protestantism of a Puritan type, and very few Catholic families were recorded: perhaps not more than a dozen. The castle and the blockhouses, constructed under Henry VIII's directions after the Pilgrimage of Grace, became fearful prisons for Catholics from all over Yorkshire. The de la Pole manor house became an arsenal, primarily for use in the Scottish wars, but in 1643 a focal point of the English Civil War. Hull had made a choice in the Pilgrimage of Grace, turning away from its Catholic past towards a prosperous Protestant future.

Further Reading:

The chapter is principally based upon the following works:

Letters and Papers, Foreign and Domestic, of the Reign of Henry VIII (1891), especially vols. 11 and 12 part i.

William Stapleton's confession in *Transactions of the East Riding Antiquarian Society*, vol. x (1903) pp. 82-105.

M. H. and R. Dodds, *The Pilgrimage of Grace and the Exeter Conspiracy* (2 vols. 1915).

A. G. Dickens, *Lollards and Protestants in the Diocese of York 1509-1558* (Oxford UP for the University of Hull, 1959).

K. J. Allison (ed.) *History of the County of York, East Riding: vol. I The City of Kingston upon Hull* (Victoria County History, 1969).

From Revolution to 'Insurrection': Hull Catholicism from the 1680s to the 1780s

by
J. Anthony Williams

'It looks like a Revolution,' wrote John Evelyn on 2 December 1688, and it must have seemed like one to the people of Hull when, two days later, anti-Catholic mobs went on the rampage and 'fell upon the Mass-house and all the houses of Papists in the Town, which they ransacked and demolished'. These excitements, part of a nation-wide outburst of 'no popery' vandalism at that time, signalled the downfall of England's last Catholic monarch, James II, after a reign lasting less than four years, and the triumph of his son-in-law, the Dutch Protestant William of Orange, whose statue is a feature of Hull's 'old town'.

From the wreckage of James's pro-Catholic policies one valuable feature did survive: at the start of his reign he had obtained for his Catholic subjects their first bishop for more than half a century, so ending an unsettled interval when, comments a contemporary report, now in the Vatican Archives, 'confirmation . . . is but a word in the catechism', and in 1687 the new bishop, Dr. John Leyburn, embarked on an extensive confirmation tour which brought him close to Hull, whose nearest priests were based in the Hedon and Burton Constable areas where Catholic survival owed much to the Constable family. Leyburn visited Burton Constable, to which confirmation candidates would have flocked from far and wide, doubtless including the Hull area.

Hull had no resident priest at that time; it was then usual for priests to travel on horseback from one Mass-centre to another and for lay people to walk or ride long distances for Mass and the sacraments – as, in a local example, from Hutton Cranswick to Everingham and back. In the late seventeenth century a leading secular priest involved with Hull was the long-serving Richard Frank, or Franks, who was in the Holderness region from the 1650s to the 1690s, overlapping initially with the future martyr Nicholas Postgate whose local link has recently been commemorated by his statue in Hornsea's Sacred Heart church. Father Frank had been appointed 'Archdeacon' of Yorkshire by the Old Chapter, a body governing the secular clergy while there was no bishop, and was instrumental in setting up the Yorkshire Brethren Fund, a clergy charity which still exists.

In the last year of James II's reign three more bishops were appointed with extensive regional responsibilities, the northern counties being entrusted to the former President of Douai College, James Smith, whose name, with those of his three episcopal colleagues, appears on a studiously non-triumphalist *Pastoral Letter to the Lay Catholics of England* which ends optimistically with the prospect of taking charge of the areas entrusted to them, and a contemporary 'newsletter' reports Bishop Smith's setting out for York (at a time when it had no Anglican archbishop), where he was warmly welcomed on 2 August and from which the 'Glorious Revolution' drove him on 22 November. He is known to have visited the East Riding later, in the very hot summer of 1710, shortly before his last illness and death. The episcopal system set up in James II's reign lasted until 1840 when the number of bishops was doubled prior to the restoration of a diocesan hierarchy ten years later, with Hull in the diocese of Beverley.

If the new bishops were far from triumphalist, the reverse was true of their enthusiastically Catholic monarch, in a hurry to improve conditions for his underprivileged and recently persecuted co-religionists. James's hasty and indiscreet policies provoked a Protestant backlash from which the East Riding's Catholics and their priests sought refuge in Hull, a garrison-town with a Catholic Governor, Lord Langdale, and some Catholic troops, but which contained few Catholic townspeople and had an unencouraging reputation and a tense atmosphere. To an earlier Governor, the Protestant Duke of Monmouth (who had led an unsuccessful rebellion against James II and paid for it with his life), attachment still lingered; in 1686 the Sheriff and his officers declined to accompany a Catholic judge to his chapel; in 1687 a Hull bookseller was suspected of handling seditious pamphlets and in June 1688 the ministers of Holy Trinity and St. Mary's, Lowgate, were reported by Langdale for their 'contempt' in refusing to read from their pulpits the King's second Declaration of Indulgence undermining the power of their own Church. In addition local resentment was aroused by the billeting of over a thousand extra troops in a town scarcely able to accommodate them and by the requirement that a man from every household should work for at least ten days on strengthening the fortifications.

But the enemy was already within and Langdale was seized 'at supper with many gentlemen and abundance of Priests', for whom, after all, the town had proved no sanctuary. Following the mob-violence against the Mass-house and buildings housing papists, the shops stayed shut, no doubt in self-protection, and the magistrates, alarmed at the excesses of 'Town Taking Day', denounced the vandalism. Above the subdued streets the colours of William of Orange flew from Holy Trinity church and on 6 December the Corporation bench-book records convivial expenditure on 'What was drunk at the Town Hall following the arrest of Lord Langdale and Catholic officers'.

The briefly glimpsed chapel disappeared and the 'refugees' dispersed, leaving behind only a handful of Catholic residents. In the preceding reign the religious census of 1676 had shown Hull to contain only three adult popish recusants (persistent absentees from Anglican services, contrary to law) and their numbers had not increased 30 years later when another count was taken. Nor did the situation improve; a limited source of information, stemming from the failed attempt to substitute James II's son for George I as King of England in 1715, relates only to propertied Catholics (whose estates had to be registered so that, if so minded, the government could confiscate two-thirds of their value) and includes no Hull residents; the only registered property in the town, a 'garden and piece of ground with the structures thereon', belonged to John Ellerker of the 'township' of Anlaby.

Twenty years later the Hull Catholics reported at the Archbishop of York's visitation of 1735 numbered but four: a widow with a young daughter, the wife of a non-Catholic mariner and a spinster. Clearly there was little promise here for the future, and in 1743 no Hull Catholics at all were reported to the next Archbishop, nor were any mentioned either then or in 1735 in the nearby parish of Sculcoates (then outside the borough). A similar sorry picture in 1745 reassured the government that Hull at least would furnish little or no Catholic support for the second rebellion in favour of 'James III'. A Northumberland farmer's son, liaising between Yorkshire Catholics and the Highland troops of the Pretender, was captured with 120 guineas on him and brought to Hull, where other reluctant Catholic visitors included French and Irish soldiers who had been captured at sea *en route* to assist the rebels and who were held in the town, as were a few Spanish troops.

In Hull's healthily Catholic hinterland priests were still active and from the Nuthill/Hedon mission and from Marton, close to Burton Constable, pastoral care was forthcoming when by mid-century a brighter future slowly dawned. In the 1760s Hull Catholicism was experiencing a modest revival, the nationwide survey of 1767 estimating its adherents in and close to the town at 40-odd, ranging from a 68-year-old labourer to children and young people 'under 18'. The adults' occupations are recorded, most of them contrasting sharply with the mainly agricultural employments of their near neighbours and include a surgeon with a Catholic servant, an innkeeper, a corn merchant, a watchmaker, a cutler and a 'whitesmith' (a worker in metal) as well as others serving the fashions of the time: a barber, two dancing masters, a milliner, a staymaker and a 'hair merchant'. The then non-urban parishes of Marfleet and Sculcoates now contained several Catholic labourers and another was reported at Sutton, together with a farmer and a grocer. The nearest Catholic teacher, the only one in the East Riding, appears to have been a schoolmistress, Elizabeth Wheelhouse, at Hedon, though in York the old-established Bar Convent was available.

Many of the Hull Catholics of 1767 were relatively recent arrivals (within the last dozen years) and no-one's residence extended back as far as 1745. Here then was the nucleus of a Catholic community, perhaps assisted from time to time by one of the priests associated with the Nuthill/Hedon mission in the late 1760s and early 1770s: James Watson, a colleague named Maire, and then Thomas Ferby, who in March 1774 started to keep a baptismal register which contains a few Hull entries. 1774 was the year in which there died at Hull, after more than two years in the town, Father James Taylor, formerly at Marton, and it was his successor there, Dr. Charles Howard, who forged a longer-lasting connection with Hull, initially foreshadowed by his stated intention to record in his mission register 'all the children baptised in the congregation of Marton . . . and adjacent towns and villages . . . and also . . . those born in the town of Kingston upon Hull from the 15th of Aug. 1774'. Father Howard, who had previously spent a short time as a riding priest in the York area, had been educated at the English Catholic house of higher studies, St. Gregory's, in Paris, and had been awarded a Sorbonne doctorate in divinity – a distinguished pastor for the people of Hull, described by one contemporary as 'very learned, agreeable, pleasant and dignified', though another, who dined with him at Harrogate in 1788 (after Howard had spent nearly 20 years in rural Holderness) was 'surprised to find the Parisian Doctor rusticated into the farmer and the learning of the Sorbonne laid aside for that of the plough'. Decidedly relaxed attitudes are glimpsed in his register, which contains loose entries on the backs of sermon-notes and of a Hull draper's bill, a revealing book-list (16 volumes of English poets, Milton, Butler's *Hudibras*, Prior and Gay as well as the Catholics Dryden and Pope) and specimens of childish penmanship: a copperplate copy of the register's title-page and, repeatedly, the incomplete line, 'The Angels did Rejoice with . . .', written by master Jonathan Youle. Father Howard rode into Hull every month or so to say Mass and doubtless to hear confessions and perhaps to catechise the children (an important activity possibly hinted at by the juvenile handiwork in his register) as well as paying occasional visits to carry out christenings or other duties.

Since no public chapel existed in Hull in the early days of his ministry it may be supposed that Father Howard followed the practice traditional to 18th-century urban Catholicism of adapting a private room (often, appropriately enough, an upper room) for the celebration of Mass, in which the keynote would have been simplicity both in surroundings and in liturgy. To such austere places of worship came congregations deeply appreciative of the Mass (and possibly Vespers) and the sacraments, some of them perhaps assisted by John Gother's *Holy Mass in Latin and English* and his participatory *Instructions and Devotions for hearing Mass*, both frequently reprinted during the 18th century, or by Bishop Challoner's long-surviving *Garden of the Soul* and many more spiritual works by him and others. For those unable to read, the rosary was a recommended devotion, often recited privately during Mass. Still-existing copies of these old books may record family information (e.g. births and deaths) dating from long before the relevant mission registers.

A leading member of Father Howard's Hull congregation appears to have been an apothecary listed in local trade directories, Reginald Williams by name, with an eminent priest-uncle and a son who entered the historic missionary college at Lisbon. He was one of the 73 Catholics who gathered in Hull to take the oath required under the very limited Catholic Relief Act of 1778; most can be traced to East Riding parishes but another Hull name is that of Thomas Fawcett, a schoolmaster (so described in Father Howard's register, and formerly of York). By this time, judging from local returns to the nationwide 'census' of papists drawn up in 1780, the number of Catholics in and near to Hull, and therefore Father Howard's flock, was in the region of 80 and a similar near-doubling since 1767 (from 7 to 15) had occurred in the extensive parish of Sutton stretching across his route from Marton to Hull.

The 1778 Relief Act represented but one small step towards rolling back more than two centuries of oppressive legislation: it meant that priests no longer risked life-imprisonment or harassment by reward-hungry informers, that Catholic teachers had greater freedom and that Catholics could purchase land and inherit it without the possibility of it being claimed by a non-Catholic relative, but oath-taking did not guarantee immunity from many other burdens originally intended (like the stones that pressed Margaret Clitherow to death in York) to crush the life out of the Catholic body. Every kind of 'Romish' religious practice, and even possession of prayer books and devotional objects, was still officially banned, though often (but not always) unofficially tolerated. Financial penalties might still be incurred for absence from the services of the Established Church – as with two Yorkshire labourers in the 1780s – and more systematically, through double taxation, threatening the economic base of the English mission and imperilling support for the numerous English monasteries, colleges and convents on the Continent. Catholics were still obliged to disclose details of their title deeds and wills (to reveal bequests for 'superstitious uses') and of any income from property in case the government decided to penalise them – as it had done, to the tune of £100,000, on top of double taxation, in 1723. Their best horses and weapons might be seized and overseas travel be restricted, and they remained excluded from some professions (hence the alternative careers of two Langdales who 'went into trade': Joseph, master of a Hull vessel, and Thomas, owner of a London distillery). The universities were closed to Catholics, as were both Houses of Parliament (and, consequently, political careers) and they were denied the vote.

However, in the very year of the Relief Act, perhaps emboldened by thoughts of better times ahead, Father Howard enlisted the aid of a well-disposed Hull solicitor and increasingly prominent local figure, Josiah Prickett, to acquire a site in Posterngate formerly occupied by a joiner's

The Posterngate Chapel, 1780 (Diocese of Middlesbrough).

workshop and here he established a new but short-lived chapel (too short-lived to appear on any near-contemporary plan of Hull), described at the time as 'a small Mass-house, newly fitted up' and later as 'a small apartment with a coved ceiling'. But the 1778 Act did not at once usher in the hoped- for better times; indeed it precipitated the anti-Catholic 'Riots of Eighty' so described and vividly portrayed by Dickens in *Barnaby Rudge*, of which a highlight, in more senses than one, is the blazing inferno of Langdale's distillery. The week-long disturbances which reduced parts of the capital to near-anarchy arose from a campaign spearheaded by the unstable Lord George Gordon to repeal the 1778 Relief Act, claiming that the government and the King (the much maligned George III who took very seriously the royal governorship of the Church of England) were intent on 'bringing in popery' – allegations coarsely cartooned and copiously expressed in print and, among numerous other such effusions, in a scrawled staccato note proclaiming 'Lord George Gordon forever. No Popery. Down with it. George the 3rd is a Roman Catholic. Dethrone him or he will massacre you all.' The government, in passing the Relief Act, had far outpaced a public opinion still infused with a longstanding and deep-seated anti-Catholicism which, heightened by the recent partnership of two Catholic powers, France and Spain, against an England hard-pressed in the War of American Independence and an invasion-scare in the summer of 1779, could readily envisage the Pope setting foot in this country – a phobia illustrated by the story of a man alleged to be the Pope 'because he lodged on St. James's Parade (close to Bath's new, and burning, Catholic Chapel) and had a night-gown with gold flowers in it'.

In Hull another gold-clad figure, the recently gilded equestrian statue of William III, 'Our Great Deliverer', symbolised the powerful Protestant leanings of the second of the two provincial centres (Bath was the other) where new Catholic chapels were so badly damaged that they had to be abandoned and whence 'no popery' fanatics, according to a local priest, had conspired to combine with associates from Leeds in a descent on York after 'demolishing everything appertaining to Popery in the East Riding'; hence, no doubt, the remark in a letter from the area, 'you are certainly safer in London than here', the London rioting having then died down.

At its height, however, Hull readers could have been regaled – and some of them perhaps inspired – by reports in their nearest newspapers (those of York, there being none published in Hull at that time) of the onset and escalation of the violence, of which an early victim was the Archbishop of York, and further intelligence could have been communicated *via* road, ferry, inland waterway and coastal carrier as well as by correspondence, such as that received locally from the capital mentioning 'a Roman Catholic gent whose house (as the phrase is) they have threatened to do over'. To another letter, after the violence had erupted nearer home, the young William Wilberforce added this postscript, writing from Beverley: 'We were alarm'd last night at Hull by a mob which burnt the Catholic chapel and attempted to pull down a private house'. The letter, headed 'Monday evening', is undated but must have been written on 12 June 1780, the day after the wrecking of Father Howard's recently established chapel, and on the Tuesday, John Raines, estate steward at Burton Constable (where elaborate precautions were taken against a feared attack), reported 'The Phrenzy of the times has extended to Hull. The mob there have destroyed the Roman Catholic Chapel.' They also assailed the premises of the prominent papist Reginald Williams, endangering his wife and family. One report, from the forces responsible for law and order, plays down this attack, merely mentioning broken windows and blaming an irresolute magistracy (as in London) but another gives a somewhat different impression, telling of 'great damage . . . Mrs. Williams' life was saved by the interposition of the magistrates and she and family were escorted out of the town by guard in a coach'. Wilberforce's words perhaps suggest that the rioters may have been checked somewhat short of their 'attempted' design, whereas the chapel was later described as 'completely wrecked' – gutted but not totally demolished.

The mob, liable to melt away among the darkening side streets and alleys of the 'old town' (which then *was* Hull), reassembled on the Monday, not dispersing until about ten o'clock that night; they had proved quite beyond the control of the local constables, who had had to be reinforced by militia from the Citadel and others – all subsequently rewarded by a grateful Bench. The magistrates, 'strongly expressed to be apprehensive' of renewed violence, had stayed up all night and additional troops were in readiness to march from Newcastle. Even allowing for an appreciable degree of local over-reaction, perhaps not unconnected with reports of the recent havoc in London, these precautions reflect foreboding, prompted by what was termed at the time 'an Insurrection of the Populace', about possible implications not confined to the persons and property of Catholics. Nor was Monday evening the rioters' last fling; they turned their attention elsewhere, causing the devoted Raines to write, 'The mob have threatened us a visit at Burton' and, in the case of another East Riding mansion with Catholic associations, the Langdales' at Houghton Hall, threats became action and a party of 'no-popery' zealots set out from Hull to attack it; however, reported its chaplain, they were intercepted and turned back before they could do any damage.

Following the rioting Father Howard's immediate concerns were to obtain compensation for the loss of his chapel and to secure accommodation for some kind of replacement. In July 1780 the House of Commons had resolved *nem con* that particulars of losses and damage sustained in the 'late rebellious Insurrection' should be presented to it at the opening of the next session, the Treasury instructed the Board of Works to make such enquiries, and a large number of claims were submitted, but early in October the Board placed an advertisement in *The London Gazette* inviting further applicants to come forward between the 12th and 19th of that month. By the latter date Father Howard's claim had been put in (as had one by the Bath priest, Dom Bede Brewer, OSB) and from this point the Board of Works' own record is amplified by that of the Corporation of Hull and by a detailed statement drawn up by Father Howard's solicitor, Josiah Prickett, and published by Canon K. Coughlan in *The Hull Catholic Magazine* of March-April 1958. Father Howard's application to the Board of Works was backed by affidavits from two witnesses to the gutting of the chapel, after which the Board requested a more detailed account of the damage, then, following scrutiny of numerous claims, the Board ruled that before my grant could be made claimants should (as a very civil letter advised Father Brewer) 'apply besides for legal remedies where the same could be obtained', *i.e.* from their local authorities. This procedure, also required of Father Howard, accorded with section six of the Riot Act of 1714 which had been much misunderstood and which magistrates had been hesitant to invoke to quell the June disturbances.

Father Howard first approached the Corporation of Hull by petition, then, in consultation with a leading Northern Circuit counsel, Alan Chambre, followed a lawsuit against the mayor and two aldermen whom the corporation resolved to indemnity while informing Father Howard that his original petition was 'a matter this Corporation has no concern with'. The legal proceedings launched by Prickett, in concert with Chambre, went ahead during the Easter and Trinity terms of 1781, but it was not until a year later, after repeated calls by Prickett's London agent upon the Board of Works and the Treasury, that his client's losses, put at £78. 11s. and 'not estimated by our clerks, but seems exceedingly well attested', were made good by the Board's surveyor in August 1782 at that figure. Prickett's fees for his protracted involvement came to £21. 11s. 4d., apart from 'attendance during the course of this brief for which no particular charge is made', and on 16 August the matter was eventually settled, leaving Father Howard with a balance of £56. 19s. 8d. It is perhaps noteworthy not only that this claim escaped close official scrutiny but that the Board of Works' ledger-entry of its settlement reads: 'Howard,

The North Street Chapel, 1799. (Diocese of Middlesbrough).

Charles Esq., for damage to a building (chapel is crossed out) in Kingston upon Hull', for while registered nonconformist meeting-houses had enjoyed the protection of the law since the Toleration Act of 1689, Catholic chapels were not yet on the same footing, unless they belonged to foreign ambassadors whose redress, following outrages against their property by the London mob, was a sensitive issue on which the House of Commons had decided a month before it turned to the more complex problem of compensating British citizens.

POSTSCRIPT: Having abandoned his Posterngate premises, which were taken over and refurbished as a synagogue for Hull's Jewish community, Father Howard opened an inconspicuous chapel in a private house intriguingly close to Holy Trinity, on North Church side, virtually an extension of Posterngate; this was followed by another apartment nearby, in Church Lane (now built over) which was being used in 1788 and was followed by a further makeshift place of worship on the fourth floor of a house in Leadenhall Square (now demolished), at that time 'inhabited by very respectable people' but by the mid-19th century 'that sink of iniquity', near what is now Alfred Gelder Street. This chapel was registered in 1793 in compliance with the second Catholic Relief Act (1791) which permitted Catholic places of worship, provided they had no steeples, and removed many existing legal handicaps. The chapel's purpose was certified by three local laymen including Joseph Denton, a clock- and watchmaker of Silver Street, possibly with a daughter at the Bar Convent, and Father Howard was registered as its 'minister'. This fourth-floor chapel, perhaps daunting to the less athletic, was said to be 'but thinly attended', a congregation of only 30 being mentioned.

Father Howard's commuting connection was now coming to a close and a Hull-based successor was about to take over in the person of an energetic and generous refugee-priest from revolutionary France, one of many who left their mark on English 'parish' life. He was the Abbé Pierre François Foucher, who had been ministering to the congregation of Pocklington and who set about providing what Father Howard had sought prematurely to establish, a public Catholic chapel. It was situated in North Street (then just that) on the outskirts of the rapidly expanding town, close to the convergence of the Beverley highway and Spring Row, the beginning of Spring Bank. Dedicated to Ss. Peter and Paul, it was opened in 1799 and was later recorded as having a Sunday service at 10.00 am and another at half past two in winter and 3.00 pm in summer. This was in 1823, two years after Father Howard's death at Marton, aged 80, and six years before its replacement by the more central church of St. Charles Borromeo (initially of very austere appearance) in 1829, the year of Catholic Emancipation which was to enable the zealous Catholic Charles Langdale, truly an Eminent Victorian, to become Member of Parliament for Beverley in 1832, signalling Catholic attainment of full citizenship and political equality.

Sources

Most relevant documents and printed works are noted in my articles (copies in Hull Local Studies Library), 'No Popery Violence in 1688: Revolt in the Provinces' in *Studies in Seventeenth Century English Literature, History and Bibliography* (ed. G. A. M. Janssens & F. G. A. M. Aarts, Amsterdam, 1984) and 'Hull, Burton Constable and the Gordon Riots' in *Northern Catholic History* no. 38 (Newcastle, 1997). The following references appertain chiefly to added material, in the sequence in which it occurs in this chapter. Vatican Archives' report: *Clergy Review*, Sept. 1935, p.194. Burton Constable confirmations: *Bishop Leyburn's Confirmation Register of 1687* (ed. J. A. Hilton and others,

Wigan, 1997). Hutton Cranswick/Everingham: *Catholic Record Society*, vol. 7, pp.260-1. Yorkshire Brethren: D. Kirkwood, *History of the Society of Yorkshire Brethren* (Leeds, 1990). *Pastoral Letter:* British Library, refs. T763(29); 108.f.62. 'Newsletter': Historical Manuscripts Commission, *12th Report, Appendix, part 5*, vol.2, p.120. Bishop Smith: B. Hemphill, *Early Vicars-Apostolic of England* (1954). Town Hall toast: Hull City Record Office, BRB6, p.231. Hull and the '45: *Yorks. Archaeological Journal*, 52, pp. 140-1. Elizabeth Wheelhouse, schoolmistress: Borthwick Institute, York, Bp. Rec. Ret. 1767/B/13; also B/10 for Maire, a Jesuit (as 'Mr. George Mayor') and, for local priests, L. Gooch, *Paid at Sundry Times: Yorkshire Clergy Finances in the 18th Century* (Ampleforth, 1997). Catholic worship etc.: J. D. Crichton, *Worship in a Hidden Church* (Dublin, 1988). Thomas Fawcett, schoolmaster: J. C. H. Aveling, *Catholic Recusancy in York* (1970) pp.139, 146, 278. Anti-Catholic legislation: *New Catholic Encyclopaedia*, 11, pp.62-5. Yorks. labourers' fines: Charles Butler, *Historical Memoirs . . .* (1822 edn.), 3, pp.276-7. Langdales in trade: Aveling, *Post-Reformation Catholicism in E. Yorks.* (1960) p.56. Joseph Denton: *Hull & Beverley Directory, 1791-2*, p.19. Bar Convent (Eliza Denton admitted 1806): H. J. Coleridge, *St. Mary's Convent, Micklegate Bar, York* (1887) p.396. Pre- and Post-1793 places of worship: *Victoria County History, Yorks.*, vol. 1, pp.331-2 (1966 list). *Note:* A recent general survey of post-Reformation Catholicism in the British Isles is Dr. Michael Mullett's *Catholics in Britain and Ireland, 1559-1829 (1998).*

Irish Immigration into Mid-Nineteenth-Century Hull

by
Jo Gibbons

At the beginning of the nineteenth century there were no more than 40 members of the Catholic Church in Hull. These numbers gradually increased and, after the passing of the Catholic Emancipation Act, the new church of St. Charles Borromeo was opened in Hull on 29 July, 1829. By 1834 the average attendance at Sunday Mass at St. Charles was said to be 450.

The National Religious Census, taken on 30 March 1851, indicated that on Census Day the attendance figures for the two services at St. Charles Catholic church (the only one at that time in Hull and Sculcoates) were:

Morning Service: 1,200 persons
Evening Service: 850 persons

This represented a significant increase in the number of Catholics since the beginning of the century. The major contributing factor to this rise was the influx of first- and second-generation Irish Catholic immigrants to the town.

Even before the Great Famine in Ireland, which began in 1845 and was the catalyst for the mass emigration of thousands of destitute Irish people, there is evidence that some Irish immigrants had already settled in Kingston upon Hull. The 1841 census records that there were already 1,400 people resident in Hull (including East and West Sculcoates) who had been born in Ireland. It is also evident that some of the Irish immigrants had been resident in Yorkshire for many years. The McGrath family in Jackson Street, Posterngate, could have arrived in Yorkshire as early as 1827 as the first child (aged 15) was born in Ireland and the next one (aged 14) in Yorkshire. It is also interesting to note that all the 43 marriages that were recorded at St. Charles church between 1840 and 1845 show that either the bride or groom (or both) had parents still living in Ireland (see Appendix 1).

The number of Irish-born was inflated by the large number of Irish soldiers stationed in the Citadel garrison in 1841. Of the 287 army personnel, 155 (52 per cent) had been born in Ireland, and there were 50 Irish-born wives and children. By 1851 there were 373 army personnel in the garrison, of whom 87 gave their place of birth as Ireland, and 12 wives and eight children were Irish-born. An interesting example of an army family's itinerant way of life can be seen in the following census entry for a family who lived in the Citadel in 1851:

Name	Age	Occupation	Place of Birth
Andrew Whittaker	34	Army Sergeant	Tyrone, Ireland
Wife	27		Gibraltar
Son	9		Gibraltar
Daughter	7		Santa Lucia, West Indies
Son	5		Canada

From the onset of the Irish Potato Famine in 1845 the number of Irish immigrants arriving in Hull significantly increased. Disembarking in Liverpool, they often moved by short 'hops' to other parts of the country, as they sought employment. In the 1851 census many of the Irish-born heads of households in Hull had children who had been born in different parts of England, as can be seen in the following example:

Mr. and Mrs. Cooley, living in Middle Street, were both born in Ireland but their eldest child (aged 10) was born in Middlesex, their next child (aged 7) in Deptford, their next son (aged 4) in Middlesex, and their two youngest children in Hull.

The St. Charles' Marriage Records confirm the increase in Irish-born immigrants after the commencement of the Potato Famine. As can be seen in Table 1, between 1846 and 1855 there were 336 marriages recorded, and of those 177 (53 per cent) show that either the bride or groom (or both) had parents still living in Ireland. These figures may, of course, be even greater because some parents may have emigrated with their children and, although their addresses at the time of marriage were given as Hull, they could have been born in Ireland.

By using the place of residence of the Irish parents of the brides and grooms, it was possible to produce a cartographical picture of patterns of immigration. Map 1 shows that the majority of immigrants came from the west of Ireland, particularly the counties of Mayo and Sligo, and, to a lesser extent, Roscommon, Leintrim and Clare.

TABLE 1: Statistics for Marriages officiated at St. Charles church between 1846-1855 indicating those brides and/or grooms who had parents still living in Ireland. (*Source: St. Charles' Marriage Records*).

YEAR	Total Number of marriages	Total number of marriages where the Bride and/or Groom still had parents living in Ireland	Percentage of Total
1846	17	10	58.8
1847	22	8	36.3
1848	33	15	45.5
1849	34	19	55.9
1850	42	26	61.9
1851	45	22	48.9
1852	55	28	50.9
1853	33	21	63.6
1854	25	17	68.0
1855	30	11	36.6

Living conditions for the Irish immigrants were often grim, and the majority lived in abject poverty. In Howard's Row, on Sutton Bank, for example, there were 20 four-roomed houses with nearly 300 people living in them – 'chiefly the low Irish'. The Irish migrants tended to congregate in particular areas. People in a strange land usually feel more comfortable living among their own countrymen, helping their neighbours and identifying with each other's problems in foreign surroundings.

There were four areas of the town where there was a high concentration of Catholics in mid-nineteenth century Hull:

AREA A: This area, close to the Railway Station, had many Lodging Houses. The area included: Mill Street, West Street, and North Street. (Of the 115 people living in Bellamy Square, Mill Street, in 1851, 94 had been born in Ireland.)

AREA B: This area, west of the River Hull, was close to the Cotton Mills, and included: Wincolmlee, Scott Street, Machell Street and Trippett Street.

AREA C: A small, overcrowded area to the east of the River Hull, known as 'The Groves'.

AREA D: This area, known as Sutton Bank, behind the Sutton Drain, had very cheap, poor housing which provided accommodation for many of the Irish immigrants before 1860.

Religion

The majority of Hull's Irish immigrants were Catholics and the *Status Animarum* of St. Charles church (a census of parishioners compiled by the clergy in 1852-53) recorded over 5,000 parishioners, 70% of whom had Irish surnames. The clergy recorded whether each person had received the three Sacraments of Confession, Holy Communion and Confirmation. These details would have indicated whether or not the inhabitants were practising Catholics, and also revealed the full extent of the priests' future missionary work. Frequently additional comments were written in the margins, such as:

> William Grady of Spring Street had 'not attended Mass for five years';

> George Middleton, living in Mary's Place, West Street, was an 'Orange Man and very bigoted' – he 'would not allow his wife Ann and stepson Peter', who were Catholics, 'to attend Mass'.

It is evident from the information contained in the *Status Animarum* that there were many Catholics at that time who were not practising their religion. Kenneth Inglis states in his work on *'Churches and the Working Class'*: 'They worshipped in one environment where it was customary to do so, and when they were set down in their new surroundings, where it was not customary for people like them to attend, they lost the habit.'

However, David Miller, in his book, *'Irish Catholicism and the Great Famine'*, argues that many of the Irish immigrants had not been regular churchgoers when they lived in Ireland. They were loyal Catholics but, particularly in Western Ireland, their religion was built around prayer in the home rather than around the Church and the priest. There had not, therefore, been the emphasis on attending Mass every Sunday.

In 1872 *The Nation* published an article entitled, *'The Irish in England'* in which Hull was singled out as the town where the largest proportion of Irish were 'fallen and lost'. It stated:

> 'Hull is the only town I have known where whole families have separated themselves in idea and sentiment from their kindred and reneges to Faith and Fatherland'.

Stereotypes

Whatever their background, the Irish tended to be lumped together and collectively referred to as 'ignorant', 'dirty' and 'primitive', and became convenient scapegoats for the many urban social problems of the day. This

Walton Court, Wincolmlee – typical housing of Irish immigrants.
(Kingston upon Hull City Council)

attitude was exacerbated by the fact that Hull was a predominantly Protestant town – in the early part of the nineteenth century there had been many 'No-Popery' campaigns and periodic anti-Catholic demonstrations in the town.

Particularly during the Famine period, the Irish immigrants were often associated with 'Famine Fever'. E. F. Collins, the Hull editor, wrote in the *Hull Advertiser* in 1847 that the influx of Irish poor was threatening to lead to serious consequences. He reported that many of the immigrants were affected with endemic diseases and the children were suffering from smallpox, whooping cough, measles and other 'contagious diseases'. This led, not unnaturally, to a general fear that the town was being overrun by hordes of fever-ridden, starving Irish.

Another common belief was that all the Irish were addicted to alcohol but, during his tour of Ireland in 1853, Collins wrote that he had 'not witnessed one case of intoxication or met a driver of a public conveyance who would not serve as an example of temperance in England'. He noted that 'most of his fellow travellers had formed their ideas of the character of Irish drivers from the representation of them on the stage and assumed that they would find them either fighting or drinking whisky in every village'.

However, there was a comparative absence of conflict in the case of the Irish in Hull even though 'the conditions and climate of opinion appeared to favour such an attack'. Graham Davis, in his article *'Little Irelands'*, attributes this to the presence of three key Irish-born, Roman Catholic individuals in Hull who occupied positions of influence and authority. These were the editor of the *Hull Advertiser*, Edward Francis Collins – who always championed the cause of the Irish in his newspaper; the local surgeon, Owen Daly; and Andrew McManus, who was the Chief Constable of the Hull Police from 1836 to 1866. Davis maintains that the presence of these three Irishmen, in positions where sensitive handling of policy and opinion were essential, 'ensured that the Irish in Hull were not made the subject of scapegoat abuse as in some other areas'.

Another key person was the Reverend Michael Trappes, Parish Priest at St. Charles church (1848-1873). His obituary, which appeared in the *Eastern Morning News* in June 1873, recalled that at the time of his appointment the town 'did not look on a Catholic with a kindly eye,' but that enemies of Catholics could not withstand Fr. Trappes' influence, and that many of his once opponents were afterwards proud to be numbered among his personal friends'.

These key figures formed the nucleus of a small but influential Irish Catholic middle-class who showed sympathy for, and an understanding of, the Irish. They were each in office for a considerable period of time which would have engendered stability in the attitudes of the host population towards the Irish and sometimes they were able to act corporately on behalf of the Irish immigrants in the town.

Employment

The principal consideration for the Irish immigrants was the possibility of obtaining work. By the mid-nineteenth century, Hull was expanding economically and there were opportunities for relatively well-paid employment. The Report on the State of the Irish Poor of 1836 concluded that 'the Irish had been, and were most efficient workmen'.

The most common means of earning a living, once the Irish reached the urban centres, was selling cheap goods. Hull was no exception as there were 51 Irish-born hawkers recorded in the town in 1841 (41 men and 10 women). The majority of Irish immigrants, both male and female, entered the lowliest, least healthy and lowest-paid of British urban occupations. They were not always welcome and were frequently treated with antagonism by their fellow workers as the immigrants represented cheap labour and a threat to the established workforce as they would often work for long hours and for low pay

By far the most important industry to be established in Hull at that time was cotton spinning and weaving. Two mills were established in the town: the Hull Flax and Cotton Mill in the Groves district in 1836 and the Kingston Cotton Mill in Cumberland Street in 1845. The workforce was almost entirely composed of new arrivals to the town, the majority of whom were from Ireland and the cotton districts of Lancashire and Cheshire. The 1841 Census for Hull recorded 26 Irish-born females and 19 Irish-born males employed in the cotton industry. Eleven of the females were 15 years or under, including: Catherine McNulty, aged 11, and Margaret Brook, aged 12, both living in the Sutton Bank area.

The majority of the 490 Irish-born occupied males (aged 14 years and over) living in Hull in 1841 were employed in the unskilled sector, but there were some skilled workmen: 15 tailors, 13 shoemakers and 11 joiners are listed. There were also: two policemen, nine men employed by HM Customs, two priests, two teachers and a surgeon – Thomas Buchanan, aged 30, who lived in Mytongate. At the other end of the spectrum there were four Irish men living in an asylum and five were in prison. The 86 Irish-born occupied females in 1841 were mainly employed in the cotton factories or domestic service. However, there were two nurses, one dressmaker, one music teacher, one furrier and even a painter.

In 1851 many of the Irish-born males were employed as dock labourers.

In mid-century very few of the dockers were in regular work and even in the busiest times were unlikely to work more than three days a week. The summer pay was 3d. (just over 1p) an hour and the winter pay 4d. The St. Charles' *Status Animarum* provided some information regarding the wages earned by the parishioners. The highest wage recorded was 18s. (90p) per week earned by Henry McDonnell, a blacksmith, living in Engine Street.

Children at Work
Remarkably few Irish children were reported as having a job. The 1841 census shows five children of Irish origin in employment, one 12-year-old boy who was a labourer; and four girls, two aged 13, who were servants, and one 12-year-old and one 11-year-old who worked in the cotton factory.

By 1853 the *Status Animarum* included the names of 1,598 Catholic children, a considerable number of whom were first- or second-generation Irish. 130 of the children had occupations, 49 girls and 82 boys. The youngest, six-year-old William Durkin's occupation was described as 'chips'; and Mary Ann Brannon, also six years, was a 'cadger' or beggar. The wages of only two of the children have been recorded: Patrick Dowd, aged 11, earned 5s. (25p) per week in a factory but Ann Judge, aged 13, also working in a factory only earned 2s. 6d. (12.5p) per week. However, it was good to read that one 13-year-old boy, William McDonald, had obtained a job in the office of the *Hull Advertiser*. The Editor was also a parishioner of St. Charles and it could be that the priest himself had put in a good word for the boy.

Education
St. Charles church, opened in 1829, was built to incorporate a schoolroom below the church, and throughout the nineteenth century the provision of a Catholic education was given priority by the Catholic community. Of the 1,598 children (785 boys and 813 girls) of school age (4-12 years) recorded in the *Status Animarum*, only 259 were attending school. A further 44 young people (between the ages of 13-19) attended Sunday School. Against each name the priest has recorded whether the individual could read or write.

An interesting factor, gleaned from the St. Charles' census, was that many of the parents with Irish surnames could read and write, but their children could not. This could have been due to the parents' inability to pay the small amounts charged for education. (The *Status Animarum* records that Martin McNamara, living in Mill Street in 1852, would not send his children to school because it cost 2d. per week). The comparatively high incidence of literacy amongst the adult Irish is probably due to the establishment of the national school system in Ireland in 1833. By the year 1845 Ireland had 3,429 schools attended daily by 433,844 pupils (*Hull Advertiser*). This fact would probably account for the large proportion of literate adults in the Irish immigrant population.

Under the direction of Fr. Trappes, two further Catholic schools were built. In 1858 St. Mary's School was opened in Wilton Street to serve the children living east of the River Hull (many of whom were the children of Irish-born cotton workers living in the Groves district), and in 1872 St. Patrick's School in Mill Street was opened 'for the use of the dense Irish population in that area'. Thus the possibility of a Catholic schooling was available to all those Irish immigrants who sought such an education.

Household Size
The Irish household size was frequently swelled by co-resident kin, lodgers and visitors. This is particularly evident in the details contained in the 1851 census. The Report by the Select Committee on the state of the Poor in Ireland commented that the willingness of the Irish to share their poverty with others even worse off than themselves was proverbial and applied both to kin and non-kin. An obligation to provide full support for an aged parent was frequently also extended to brothers, sisters, aunts and uncles, and their children if destitute orphans. Examples are given below:

> Michael Lyons and his wife, living at 16 Mill Street, had their two children, four cousins (aged 16-18 years) and a widowed lodger and her daughter living with them. They all gave their place of birth as Ireland and, as the youngest child was only three, it is highly likely that they had been in Ireland at the time of the Famine.

> James and Ellen Bolton, a young couple living in Bellamy Square, had the husband's three brothers and two sisters living with them, ranging in age from 8-20 years.

The incidence of Irish households with lodgers was high in 1851 and the number varied significantly from Susan McIntyre, a widow, living in Mill Street, who had only one lodger – another widow (aged 70 years) – to the occupants of 4 Mill Street, John Loftus and his wife had six children, a servant and 25 lodgers living with them.

Law and Order
It was a common belief in Victorian Britain that the Irish were responsible for much of the crime and disorder in the country and that they were

more criminal than other sections of British society. In 1841 there were 135 prisoners in Hull Gaol, of whom eight per cent were Irish-born – nine males and two females. By 1851 there were 21 Irish-born prisoners (17 male and 4 females) this being 13 per cent of the total of 162. It was recorded that many of the newly-arrived and destitute Irish committed petty misdemeanours merely to obtain a bed for the night (it would have had the advantage of being less terrible than either Ireland in the Forties or the Hull Workhouse). These figures would not substantiate the claim that the Irish were responsible for most of Hull's crime.

Poor Law – drain on the Rates

A further factor that could have led to antagonism towards the Irish was that they were widely believed to be a burden on the Poor Rates. There is no evidence that this was true of the pre-Famine settled Irish-born population of Hull. The 1841 Census shows that none of the 227 residents of Hull Workhouse had been born in Ireland, and only six (3.2 per cent) of the inmates of Sculcoates Workhouse were Irish-born.

In the immediate pre-Famine period the small Irish community differed little from the rest of Hull's population, but with the influx of the Famine victims in the mid-Forties, attitudes began to change. Reports of Irish vagrancy, deaths in the Workhouse, disease, drunkenness and petty theft increased with the continuous flow of immigrants into the town, and this alarmed local residents.

There is evidence of discrimination against the Irish by the Poor Law authorities. For example, in 1844 there was great overcrowding in Hull Workhouse and, to reduce the congestion, 50 Irish inmates, most of whom had worked in Hull for many years, were deported to Dublin. The Governor of the Poor chose to ignore the law that no settled person could be removed, still less deported. More would have been sent but for the intervention of Fr. Render, incumbent of St. Charles, and the condemnation in the press, led by E. F. Collins of the *Hull Advertiser.*

However, the number of vagrants temporarily relieved by the Hull Vagrant Office did rise dramatically: from 1,489 in 1846 to 4,035 in 1847. It must be assumed that this was a direct result of the influx of destitute Irish escaping the Famine. Mr. Drant, Governor of Hull Workhouse, said that the greater portion of the additional vagrants were Irish, and that during 1847 they had 'interred 105 adults and 80 children belonging to the Irish who had been exposed to all kinds of wind and weather and had suffered privations and want of food and were in a very bad state'. He went on to say that they frequently had a number of children, and if they were ill the following morning they were obliged to keep them until the children recovered. However, many of them died. A total of 90 adults and 32 children under ten years of age, many of whom were Irish, died in the Workhouse that year.

The post-Famine immigrants would have been starving, destitute and therefore weak and ill even before they left their homeland. They were not local paupers temporarily out of work, but people who had often walked from town to town looking for employment and shelter. When they arrived in Hull, because of its geographical position, there was nowhere else to travel to. They had no alternative but to seek assistance from the Poor Law Board, and the Workhouse had to accept them or they died in the street.

However, by 1851, of the 250 inmates of the Sculcoates Workhouse only two men and two women had been born in Ireland. Of the 369 residents in Hull Workhouse there were 16 Irish-born inmates – 9 children and seven adults, of whom five were over the age of 64, one being blind and another insane.

Prejudice towards a particular section of society is a difficult concept to measure. The Irish, being poor and sometimes illiterate, have left no records of their feelings towards their non-Irish neighbours, and the latter, also being poor, have left no records of their attitudes towards the Irish immigrants. There were occasional newspaper reports of fighting between the two communities but the incidents were very different from the anti-Catholic, 'No Popery' disturbances of the early nineteenth century.

Although the Irish-born population of Hull more than doubled in the decade 1841-1851, from 1,400 to 2,893, they still only represented a small proportion of the immigrant population. In 1851, 47.2 per cent of the total population of the Borough of Hull had been born outside the Borough. It was, therefore, not just the Irish but all the migrants who would have put a strain on Hull's resources.

The Irish immigrants who came to Hull were caught in a 19th-century poverty trap. They were predominantly from the province of Conaught and, on arrival, many of the immigrants would have been suffering from the psychological effects of being uprooted from their mainly agricultural background into an urban slum environment with an alien culture and religion. They had to quickly acquire both the work and social skills of the new industrial, urban culture that they had encompassed. Many of the citizens of Hull viewed them with, at least, suspicion and, at the worst, with hatred but, if the position had been reversed and the native industrial workers and slum dwellers of Hull had been put down in a field in Connaught, they too would have been viewed with suspicion and ridiculed for their lack of the agricultural and social skills required of that community.

References

The Census Reports for Hull dated 1841 and 1851.
The Marriage Records of St. Charles church, Hull, 1839-1864.
The *Status Animarum* of St. Charles church dated 1852-53.
Copies of the *Hull Advertiser* and the *Eastern Morning News*.
Carson, R., *The First Hundred Years, A History of the Diocese of Middlesbrough 1878-1978* (Middlesbrough, 1978).
Collins, E. F., *Brief Notes of a Short Excursion to Ireland* (Hull,1853).
Davis, G., *The Irish in Britain* (Beckenham, 1985).
Gilley, S. and Swift, R., *The Irish in the Victorian City* (1985).
Sheahan, J. J., *History of the Town and Port of Kingston upon Hull* (Beverley, 1866).

APPENDIX 1

Date of Marriage	Names of Bride and Groom	Addresses of Bride/Groom	Names of Parents	Parents' Place of residence
2.3.1840	Joseph Mallet	Hull	Thomas & Mary Mallett	Co. Mayo, Ireland
	Mary Dine	Hull	William & Mary Dine	Manchester
4. 8.1840	Patrick O'Conner	Sutton Bank	Michael & Mary O'Conner	Ireland
	Bridget McNaulty	Sutton Bank	Anthony & Cath. McNaulty	Hull
7.9.1840	Patrick Nicholson	Collier Street	John & Mary Nicholson	Co. Sligo, Ireland
	Ann Lundy	Collier Street	James (dead) and Margaret Lundy	Hull
6.11.1840	Peter McCue	Middle Street	Thomas & Mary McCue	Ireland
	Margaret Agan	Mill Street	Michael & Margaret Agan	Mill Street, Hull
26.1.1841	Thomas Foy	West Street	Michael & Bridget Foy	Co.Mayo, Ireland
	Bridget Maxwell	West Street	Patrick & Bridget Maxwell	Co. Sligo, Ireland
6.7.1841	Thomas Wilson	Mill Street	Wm. & Dorothy Wilson	Morpeth
	Mary McAlister	Mill Street	Bernard McAlister	Co. Down, Ireland
12.7.1841	Michael McCourt	Waterworks St.	Cormack & Bridget McCourt	Fermanagh, Ireland
	Mary McQuillan	Mill Street	Arthur & Cath. McQuillan	Fermanagh, Ireland
11.8.1841	Charles McAllister	Mill Street	Charles & Helen McAllister	Ireland
	Mary Wilson	Mill Street	Patrick & Ann Wilson	Ireland
25.10.1841	John Welsh	Mill Street	Richard & Bridget Welsh	Ireland
	Mary Dowd	Mill Street	Patrick and Ann Dowd	Mill Street
12.11.1841	Thos. Masterman	Sutton Bank	John & Mary Masterman	Ampleforth
	Margaret Mooney	Sutton Bank	David & Margaret Mooney	Ireland
13.2.1842	Patrick Peacock	Garrison	James & Margaret Peacock	Ireland
	Mary Peacock	Drypool	Thos. & Ann Peacock	Ireland
10.8.1842	John Ralph	Garrison	Andrew & Marg. Ralph	Carlow, Ireland
	Ann Brislett	Drypool	Thos. & Sarah Brislett	Lincolnshire
1.11.1842	Thomas Neylons	Edward Street	James & Cath. Neylons	Co. Sligo, Ireland
	Mary Deaning	North Street	Thos. & Jane Dearing	North Street, Hull
23.1.1843	Bernard Finnarty	Mill Street	Michael & Bridget Finnarty	Ireland
	Mary Cranston	Mill Street	John & Grace Cranston	
29. 1.1843	Patrick Ansbrough	Mill Street	John & Mary Ansborough	Ireland
	Anne Crane	Mill Street	William & Mary Crane	Ireland
13.11.1843	Edward McGrath	Mill Street	John & Ann McGrath	Dublin, Ireland
	Catherine Wogan	Mill Street	George & Mary Wogan	Mill Street, Hull

12.12.1843	Michael Gilsee	Mill Street	Donal & Cath. Gilsee	Co. Sligo, Ireland
	Anne Smith	Mill Street	John & Bridget Smith	Mill Street, Hull
27.12.1843	William Hinds	North Street	William Hinds	Co. Sligo, Ireland
	Mary Murphy	West Street	Daniel Murphy	Sutton Bank, Hull
17.11.1844	Owen McGuire	Mill Street	Owen & Bridget McGuire	Ireland
	Rose Ann Murphy	West Street	Hugh & Bridget Murphy	Ireland
18.1.1844	James Harrin	Mill Street	Lawrence & Bridg. Harrin	Ireland
	Bridget Gara	Mill Street	Owen & Anne Gara	Ireland
19.3.1844	Christopher Broadley	Wood's Entry	Joseph & Ruth Broadley	Leeds
	Bridget Fox	High Street	Christopher & Ellen Fox	Monaghen,Ireland
30.4.1844	Robert Reynolds	Collier Street	Thos. & Catherine Reynolds	Ireland
	Elizabeth Taylor	Mason Street	John & Sarah Taylor	Hull
17.6.1844	Patrick McCarrick	Middle Street	Thos. & Cath. McCarrick	Ireland
	Anne Hart	Mill Street	Michael & Catherine Hart	Mill Street, Hull
1.6.1844	Patrick Dempsey	Sutton Bank	Patrick Dempsey	Co. Mayo, Ireland
	Bridget Moran	Sutton Bank	James Moran	Co. Leitrim, Ireland
30. 6.1844	Cornelius Owens	Mill Street	Patrick & Ellen Owens	Westmeath, Ireland
	Margaret Meni . . .	Mill Street	Patrick & Mary Meni . . .	Co. Mayo, Ireland
27. 9.1844	Patrick Mank . . .	Mill Street	Patrick Mank . . .	Co. Leitrim, Ireland
	Bridget Harmon	Mill Street	Michael Harmon	Roscommon, Ireland
12.11.1844	Bernard McPorthen	Sutton Bank	Michael & Mary McPorthen	Ireland
	Mary Shea	Sutton Bank	Timothy & Margaret Shea	Ireland
23.11.1844	James Pearson	Hull	Thos. & Elizabeth Pearson	Leicestershire
	Ann Smith	Hull	Patrick & Cath. Smith	Queens Co., Ireland
23.11.1844	David ?	Ireland	David & ? ?	Ireland
	Jane Williams	Holderness Rd.	Wm. & Jane Williams	Holderness Rd, Hull.
8.12,1844	William Daley	West Street	John Daley	Dublin, Ireland
	Anne Varey	West Street	Michael Varey	Mill Street, Hull
8.12.1844	Thomas Smith	Citadel	Thomas Smith	Coventry
	Catherine Smith	Drypool	Patrick Smith	Co. Navan, Ireland
5. 2.1845	James Harvey	Albert Street	Patrick & Ellen Harvey	Co.Donegal, Ireland
	Mary Smith	Dun . . . Street	James & Anne Smith	Ireland
20. 5.1845	John Willis	? Street	George & Mary Wallis	Co. Mayo, Ireland
	Mary Wallis	Stubbs Bldgs.		
26. 5.1845	John Ford	Sutton Bank	John & Anne Ford	Co. Leitrim, Ireland
	Jane D . . .	Sutton Bank	Thos. & Elizabeth D . . .	Liverpool
5. 6.1845	Peter McDowell	Middle Street	Ennis & Mary McDowell	Dublin, Ireland
	Mary ?	Middle Street	Patrick & Cath. Gibson	Co. Cavan, Ireland
5. 6.1845	James Mallan	Citadel	Thomas & Mary Mallan	Co.Armagh, Ireland
	Caroline Coolman	Drypool	Michael & Mary Coolman	Leeds
16. 6.1845	James Moran	Mill Street	Patrick & Mary Moran	Co. Down, Ireland
	Bridget McAlister	West Street	Charles & Ellen McAlister	Hull
29. 7.1845	Robert Consett	Holderness Rd.	Richard & Ann Consett	Wawne
	Catherine Boyn	Sutton	John & Bridget Boyn	Ireland
29. 7.1845	David Lynch	Mill Street	Darby Lynch	Ireland
	Mary Alleney	Mill Street	Ireland	
27. 9.1845	Peter McCormack	Hull	Hugh McCormack	Monaghen, Ireland
	Jane Wood	John Wood	Lincolnshire	
6.10.1845	William Amos	Mytongate	Edward Amos	Dublin, Ireland
	Winifred Pearson	Sewer Lane	John & Margaret Pearson	Ireland
20.10.1845	William ?	Garrison	Robt. & Bridget ?	Co.Tipperary, Ireland
	?	Drypool	Connor & Cath. ?	Co.Tipperary, Ireland
19.11.1845	Michael Allen	Citadel	Peter & Margt. Allen	Ireland
	Ann Kilmartin	Drypool	Francis & Cath. Kilmartin	Ireland.

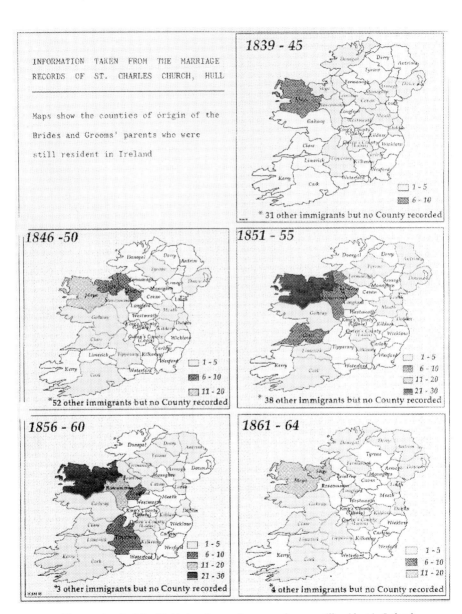

The counties of origin of brides' and grooms' parents who were still resident in Ireland.

62

The Story of the First Hull Mercy Nuns

by
Marie McClelland

In her fascinating study of *Nuns in Nineteenth Century Ireland* (Dublin 1987), Caitriona Clear upends the traditionally-held view that entering the religious life was a means of escape from the 'real world'. In an attempt to justify why so many women entered convents on such an unprecedented scale throughout the century, Miss Clear posits the view that to do so was the only career opportunity for women of talent or authority at that time. Her view is an interesting context within which to examine the work of those Irish women who were to become the first Hull Mercy nuns. The story of their endeavours shows little evidence of an escape from public affairs or of a quiet retreat into a cosy world of sheltered convent life.

The first Hull nuns entered Baggot Street Convent, Dublin, between July 1850 and February 1852, just eleven years after the death of Catherine McAuley, the foundress of the Mercy Congregation. Baggot Street had become a thriving centre for the training of nuns to service the corporal and spiritual needs of the poor, the sick and the ignorant by means of an *uncloistered* apostolate. The Mercy diaspora in the first decade of McAuley's foundation had penetrated far-flung places like Newfoundland, New York, Western Australia and Turkey as well as Liverpool, London and Cheadle nearer home. Mercy convents had also been established in many towns throughout Ireland. Those who chose to become Mercy nuns in those early days could, therefore, expect to have to leave their conventual cradle for new and distant places. Mary Starr, Susan Saurin, Julia Kennedy, Mary Agnes McOwen and Frances Delaney had scarcely settled into their Dublin convent when in 1855 they were sent to answer a call for help with the school and the parish of Fr. Edward Clifford in the village of Clifford, near Boston Spa. (Their association with Hull was to come later!) They were joined by a lay sister (Juliana Cahill), two novices (Clare King and Catherine Dixon) and a postulant (Sr. Bernard Nelligan). Mary Starr was appointed superior with Julia Kennedy as Assistant and Bursar. Starr had been a professed nun for just two years. A convert to Catholicism, she was filled with the zeal of her new vocation and her newly enriched mission in life.

Despite their infancy in terms of conventual training, these new nuns had been long enough in Baggot Street to have been imbued with the spirit of Catherine McAuley. McAuley had lived and preached a life of devoted hard work and prayer. She had a clear sense of mission which was rooted in a passionate belief in the power of women as a lever for the betterment of society. 'If wives were good,' she claimed, 'they could save their husbands; if sisters were good, they could save their brothers; if mothers were good, they could rear their children properly.' She was convinced that her Mercy nuns, being free to travel where and when needed, free to discourse with all manner of people and free to visit homes, hospitals, institutions and prisons, could begin to address this vital mission of enriching society for the greater glory of God. *'Labour as if success depended upon your own exertions,'* she urged her companions, *'but pray as though it depended upon God.'* Within two years of their coming to Clifford, Starr and her companions had learned, through experience, that the success of managing a new convent, a new school and a new apostolate could be greatly affected by the quality of relationships established between the nuns and a whole host of people external to them. Government school inspectors, Catholic benefactors, influential parishioners, local tradesmen and business people, school-children and their parents and, above all, the parish priest, all had an impact on the public image of the convent and all could influence attitudes to the nuns for better or worse. Starr was eminently conscious of her need for total trust in God to support her in her challenging rôles and she cultivated a somewhat intense, if not severe, piety as an outward sign of this trust. Being cut loose from the umbilical cord of Baggot Street Convent, she became over-zealous in the exercise of her authority as superior, resulting in the adoption of an unduly strict and spartan way of life for the Clifford nuns. This was a legacy that was carried over to and sustained in the Hull convent. Indeed, by 1893, one nun who had visited Mercy convents at Liverpool, Chelsea, Bermondsey, Guernsey and Alnwick, complained to her bishop that the Hull convent was the most austere of all of them and that the quality of food, clothing and heating there left a lot to be desired.

The Clifford nuns became the Hull nuns when Fr. Michael Trappes, priest-in-charge of St. Charles' church, wrote to Baggot Street for help to staff his proposed new school-cum-chapel on the corner of Dansom Lane/ Wilton Street in 1857. Baggot Street was drained of ready recruits and Trappes's request was thus re-directed to Clifford. Starr's community numbered 24 by then, thus enabling her to seize the opportunity to apply the wisdom of two years experience to a *'fresh start'* in what was to prove to be real mission territory. The census returns for 1841, 1851, 1861 and 1871 indicate a steady flow of immigrant Irish into Hull in common with many other major English cities. The Hull pattern amounted to 2 to 3% of the town's population each year. Bernard Kelly, in his *Historical Notes on English Catholic Missions*, estimates the congregation of St. Charles' Church in the year 1850-1 as 6,500, with 240 children attending the elementary school in its basement. Returns from the Religious Census, however, taken on Sunday, 30 March 1851, reveal no more than 1,200 attending Mass in the morning and 850 the afternoon service. While none of these sets of figures can supply a totally accurate or reliable picture of the size of the mission served by Fr. Trappes and his curate, Fr. John Motler, one thing was abundantly clear. The town needed more than one church and one school and all the personnel it could muster if it was to help to persuade the immigrants to continue in the practice of their faith and to develop a sense of belonging in their newly-adopted country. The task was a daunting one which would have scared off all but those who were strong in conviction and commitment.

Five nuns, including Starr and Kennedy, came to Dansom Lane initially, but as the school's popularity and population grew, more were drafted in from Clifford. Starr remained superior of the Hull and Clifford convents for the next 10 years with McOwen, Delaney, King and Nelligan sharing minor roles of responsibility at her behest. The nuns engaged themselves in a full range of work, in addition to teaching e.g. visiting the poor and the sick in their homes, attending to Catholics in the workhouse on Sculcoates Lane and operating a regular visiting schedule to the female wing of the prison on Hedon Road. In time, they established a 'House of Mercy' in the heart of the mills and factories district where they trained women in the art of housekeeping and hygiene. The rapid expansion of Catholic schools in Hull under the direction of the Mercy nuns from 1857 to the turn of the century is a success story of sterling worth but in its early stages some of that expansion took place at great cost to the Clifford schools. Money that could be spared from Clifford was often used to pay urgent bills in Hull. Worse still, teaching skills that were sharpened in Clifford were frequently re-deployed to Hull schools. There was considerable trafficking of nuns between the two convents with travelling expenses amounting to £20 a year. Understandably, relationships between Starr and Fr. Clifford (and his successor after 1860, Fr. John Cullimore) became severely strained. By 1867 they were quite intolerable and the whole community of nuns moved from Clifford to settle in Hull. In that year, Starr stepped down as superior in favour of Kennedy, who was to rule for the next 27 years.

Starr's departure from the helm signified the toll she paid for the pressures and strains which accompanied her success story. A written agreement signed in 1857 between Fr. Trappes and the nuns – guaranteeing them daily Mass in their convent and freedom from school expenses arising from rent, taxes, repairs, furniture, light and heating, resources and cleaning – soon proved to be worthless as the demand for school places increased and more and more of the priests' time had to be devoted to the needs of parishioners. The nuns vacated their upstairs room in the Dansom Lane premises within the first twelve months to allow for expansion of the school room. They moved into a large mansion known as Keddy's Hall on the Elm Tree Estate at the corner of Anlaby Road and South Parade. The Hull Catholic community agreed to pay the £3,800 purchase price by means of frequent fund-raising bazaars and a weekly collection in church. Meanwhile, at their own expense, the nuns converted the stables into an elementary school for girls, turned the ballroom into a nuns' chapel and the dining room into a private 'pension school' for the fee-paying daughters of the middle classes. After three years of the church collection, however, only £1,000 had been raised and Hull Catholics had lost their appetite for contributing, chiefly, one suspects, because their limited resources were overstretched. It fell to the nuns to pay off the residual £2,800, but the new curate at St. Charles' church, Fr. Arthur Riddell, insisted on reminding them of the generous £1,000 donated by the poor of Hull!

The sharp personalities of Starr and Kennedy were not altogether compatible with that of the more affable and able future bishop of Northampton, Fr. Riddell. The personal appeal of the two nuns was rendered even less attractive with the eruption, in 1869, of 'The Great Convent Case'. The court case was brought against Starr and Kennedy by the Saurin family who were greatly distressed about the indignities endured by Susan Saurin – one of the founding nuns. Such treatment, it was alleged, was tantamount to forcing Saurin to leave the convent against her will. The case was held in London, and the proceedings of the trial were minutely reported in the national and local press. So much media coverage ensured that Starr and Kennedy, too, and indeed the entire Hull contingent, suffered a good measure of public notoriety. By dint of its having hurtled a very private group of nuns into a very public limelight, in a country that was all too readily hostile to nuns, *The Great Convent Case* was a scandalous affair. Yet it must be emphasised that no scandal was uncovered in the course of the trial. Saurin won the case, thereby preserving her legal right to remain a nun in the Hull convent. She did, in fact, leave of her own volition and the memory of the trial was confined to the cupboard as a skeleton best forgotten.

The period leading up to the trial was filled with pressures and strains from episcopal visitations, an ecclesiastical Commission of Inquiry into the running of the convent, discourses and arguments, corresponding meetings with relatives, with priests, with parishioners, with doctors and lawyers and with one another. It was a period, too, when there were many minor skirmishes between the nuns and the clergy of both Hull and Clifford over issues of ownership of property and authority over schools. So much turmoil served to sap the strength of Starr while, in contrast, it fuelled the determination of Kennedy to steer her convent community into a new era of expansion and success and into a position where they would never be content to be parochial in their outlook nor circumspect in their missionary endeavours. She began by selling the Keddy's Hall mansion and estate, except for the kitchen garden plot. With the profits from the sale she returned to the Hull Catholics the £1,000 they had originally donated. On the site of the garden plot she then ordered the erection of a new purpose-built convent – always referred to as The Mother House – with its own private chapel, its own elementary school (St. Joseph's) and an adjoining secondary school (St. Mary's High School). The grand opening of The Mother House in 1873 marked a new independence for the nuns. Over the next 20 years, they set up branch convents in thirteen different locations including Carlton, Whitby, Bradford, Middlesbrough, North Ormesby, South Bank and Normanby. Three nuns volunteered to join the new Brisbane convent in Australia. In 1883, the Mercy annalist could claim that over 2,500 children were being taught by the nuns in Hull and that the numbers of professed nuns had risen to 40. Moreover, the convent had continued to attract 'home-grown' vocations, which meant that a more English corporate personality was emerging.

When Kennedy died in 1894, she was succeeded by Mother Stanislaus Dawson, a native of Epworth on the Isle of Axholme. Dawson had joined the Hull convent in 1861 and was well-crafted in the mould of the founding nuns. She shared many of the strong character attributes of Kennedy but she was a woman of much more polish and charm. Having come from an established and influential family of lawyers and priests, she knew instinctively how to handle people like church and civic dignitaries, local clergy, visiting gentry and parents, government inspectors and other professional visitors, gardeners, plumbers, architects, builders and even the Beverley Road tram conductors. Her special charism as a hard-working yet very prayerful woman is richly recorded in the four-volume handwritten diaries penned by an un-named nun from 1905-1909.

The story of the Hull nuns has always escaped the attention of serious historians and has relied for its telling on parish commemorative studies or on oral history. In the oral history of the community, Dawson emerges as the most popular of the first three superiors because of her association with Endsleigh. Thanks to Dawson's ingenuity in bidding by proxy at a public auction, Endsleigh mansion house and estate on Beverley Road were secured for the nuns in 1899. The extensive land-holding thus gained cleared the way for the building of the only Mercy teacher training college in England together with its own 'Demonstration School' (dedicated to the Holy Child) and for the development of a convent, a chapel and a private elementary school (dedicated to St. Anthony). As the new century progressed, much of the nuns' work was concentrated on this site and particularly so after The Mother House complex on Anlaby Road was bombed out in the Blitz. This led to a gradual change in nomenclature that grew out of convenience rather than from any deliberate policy. The Hull nuns became known as the *Endsleigh nuns* and their institutions as *Endsleigh College* and *Endsleigh School*.

While oral history is a powerful vehicle for immortalising people and events, it can sometimes lose sight of gradual processes and imperceptible reactions. An examination of Hull's educational history after the passing of the 1870 Education Act, shows the emergence of the Hull School Board with a somewhat 'testy' attitude towards denominational schools. The Board seemed hell-bent on enabling Hull children to avoid having to attend any one of the schools run by nuns and it opposed all applications for the expansion of existing Catholic schools in the city. When School Boards were replaced with Local Education Authorities by the 1902 Education Act, the situation did not improve. The anti-Catholic nature of the Hull Authority and particularly of its Education Committee was epitomised in the vociferous attacks on 'Popish institutions' led by Alderman Alfred Gelder and Councillor S. P. Wood. Their deliberate campaign to undermine the supply of Catholic teachers for the city by refusing to recognise the Catholic Pupil Teacher Centre run by the nuns at Anlaby Road and by refusing to support Catholic pupil-teachers who wished to train there generated lengthy reports in local newspapers and in the Local Authority minute books from 1904 to 1906. The details of that story are told elsewhere[1] but the real worth of its long-term effects is often omitted when the story of the Hull nuns is recalled.

We have seen how, from the very start of their mission to England, the nuns had to cope with a fair share of criticism from within their own ranks, from lay Catholics and from parish clergy. Yet at each stage they responded by strengthening their resolve for self-improvement without prejudice to their missionary focus. When faced, therefore, with criticisms from non-Catholics on the Hull School Board or on the Hull Local Education

Committee, their response was no different. Knowing full well that every identifiable fault in the management of their schools would provide ammunition for their opponents, they set about minimising these as much as possible. They ploughed considerable amounts of their own earnings into resources and maintenance; they improved attendance rates through their home-visiting and parish links and also by awarding annual prizes of shoes and clothing to children who had full attendance; they laid great store by employing certificated teachers wherever possible and they placed all their schools under regular government inspection. The latter move in itself guaranteed a certain standard of provision before inspectors could recommend the issuing of government grants. Thus, the Catholic schools improved and expanded as a result of and in spite of local opposition. At the same time, the determination and earnestness of the nuns evinced a new appreciation from local lay Catholics. Efforts to show this appreciation were, in turn, to develop a new public image of strength in these lay Catholics.

In May 1904, the (Hull) *Daily Mail* carried a lengthy letter exhorting 'Irishmen of Hull' to combine 'in the formation of a Citizens League' to protect their schools from the 'unquestionable attitude of determined hostility' within the Hull Education Committee. The letter was typical of a growing indignation among Catholics in the city. The call was taken up by Fr. J. Hall, the indomitable priest in charge of St. Charles', as he sought to rejuvenate Hull's branch of The Catholic Union and to bestir the city's Catholics into collective action. In his Lenten Pastoral of 1905, Bishop Lacy of Middlesbrough also attacked the Hull Education Committee for not having 'quite risen to the dignity of its responsible position' and he called upon Catholic parents everywhere to 'show a united front in defence of their educational rights'. His pastoral was read in every Catholic church in Hull and was published in full in the Hull newspapers under the title '*The Bishop of Middlesbrough and The Education Committee*'. Throughout 1904 and 1905, many public meetings were held in the city to orchestrate a response. When the time came for the local election of November 1905, Hull Catholics had been galvanised into a forceful and corporate group who were ready to use the power of the ballot box to effect a change in the people who represented them in public office. Immigrant and local native Catholics had been assimilated in the process and they could thus look forward to a more confident future arising from a greater sense of belonging.

For their part, the nuns moved into a new realm of educational challenge with the establishment of Endsleigh Training College in September 1905. New demands were made of them to gain university qualifications themselves and to employ a wide variety of well-qualified lay staff to ensure a steady supply of Catholic teachers over the next 70 years. The story of the development of the college[2] testifies yet again to women who 'laboured as if success depended upon (their) own exertions but prayed as though it depended on God'.

Catherine McAuley used to like to empower her emissaries, as they set off for new horizons, with the following piece of advice: 'Do not become overwhelmed with the enormity of your task. Remember it is God's work you are engaged in, not your own'. The Hull nuns proved to be shining examples of this advice in action. The fruits of their labours in establishing firm roots for Catholic schools have left a valuable legacy to the Catholics of Hull. On the eve of the Third Millennium, therefore, it behoves the Catholics of Hull to preserve and nurture those schools and to refuse to be overwhelmed by arguments of rationalisation and financial exigencies which may eventually threaten to effect their closure. Such an outcome would surely amount to vandalism when mirrored against the struggles of the Mercy nuns who engaged themselves so outstandingly in God's work in this city.

The term 'nun' is used throughout this chapter for brevity's sake and because it is the term most popularly used to describe women religious. It is acknowledged that, canonically speaking, a nun is a strictly enclosed religious.

1. See my chapter on 'Catholic Education in Victorian Hull' in Gilley & Swift (eds): *The Irish in Victorian Britain* (Four Courts Press, Dublin, 1999).
2. The full study of the work of the Hull nuns is to be published by the Edwin Mellen Press in 1999 in my book: *The Growth of a Community: Nuns, Religion & Politics in Nineteenth-Century Hull*.

Edward Francis Collins, 1807-1872
Hull's Catholic Victorian Crusader

by
Jo Gibbons

In January, 1872, the death took place in London of a retired journalist who apparently had few friends or relatives in London, as only his wife and one other mourner attended his funeral. Yet this man, Edward Francis Collins, had, for twenty-four years (1841-1866) been the much respected editor of the *Hull Advertiser*. His obituary in the *Eastern Counties Herald* states that Collins was able to influence public opinion by his 'bold and uncompromising advocacy', and that 'no man in Hull, before or since, wielded so much power as he or wielded it so well or so wisely'. This was high praise for the editor of a provincial newspaper who had arrived as a stranger to the town with no local connections, and who did not have the advantages of wealth or position.

Edward Francis Collins was born in County Donegal in 1807 and, according to a volume of biographical notes of *Eminent Temperance Reformers*, he showed intellectual promise from an early age. In 1831 he went to London with letters of introduction to several members of the House of Commons, including Joseph Hume, who appointed him as his private secretary. Once in London, and in his confidential position, Collins had ample opportunity to meet with the leading reformers of the day and to explore the wider world of radical politics.

In 1834 Hume encouraged Collins to become one of the sub-editors of the *Sun* newspaper, then one of the most enterprising London daily journals; and also advised him to read law with an eminent barrister with a view to adopting law as a profession. However, a dislike of speaking in public and the dread of the precariousness of a young lawyer's prospects without friends to support him led him to abandon his law training and he was never called to the Bar.

In 1841 Collins left London to become the editor of the *Hull Advertiser*, a weekly newspaper that promoted the Liberal cause. Collins' appointment was paradoxical as he was a known Radical and a staunch Roman Catholic, yet, only ten years earlier, the editor and proprietor of the *Hull Advertiser*, Isaac Wilson, had been a Tory with staunch anti-Catholic feelings.

Collins was determined to raise the status of the provincial press and set about the task with his customary earnestness and great intellectual ability. John Leng, who served his journalistic apprenticeship under Collins, later wrote of his admiration for the rare ability of his former employer and remarked on 'his extraordinary erudition, varied scholarship and humorous illustrations which made his writings so conspicuous in provincial journalism'. Collins was tireless in his pursuit of justice for the underprivileged, and strongly criticised local anti-Jewish and anti-Catholic prejudice.

The mid-19th century was a period of great transformation and change in Hull. Industrialisation, increased population and acceleration in urbanisation led to many social and economic problems. The poor flocked to Hull in search of work and lived in appalling conditions. It soon became evident, to those with a social conscience, that something had to be done to tackle Hull's many environmental, social and economic problems.

Much of the initiative and publicity for the many controversial social issues of the day, such as the investigation into Hull's sanitary conditions, poor law agitation, the campaign to close Charity Hall and replace it with a newly built workhouse, and the drainage controversy of the 1850s, can be traced to the work of Edward Francis Collins. He was ably assisted in his campaigns by many men who held similar views to himself. One social issue which was particularly close to Collins' heart was the welfare of the Irish immigrants who sought refuge in Hull, and particularly the plight of the Irish people during the time of the Great Famine 1845-1848.

Although the majority of the mass migration from Ireland in the Victorian era came from the labouring and tenant-farmer classes, some of the immigrants were intellectuals who turned to journalism on arrival in England. They established Catholic publications such as *The Tablet* (1840), and the most successful Catholic paper, *The Universe* – its price of 1d. meant that it reached a wide Catholic audience. However, it was individual Irish Catholics working on secular provincial journals, such as Edward Francis Collins, who won more attention for Ireland. This was undoubtedly true during the period of the Irish Potato Famine.

The Irish Famine was the most appalling disaster, not only in Irish history, but in the history of 19th-century Europe. By the 1840s the potato was the sole food of many of the Irish people, and when the potato blight struck in 1845 the results were catastrophic. Out of a total population of 8½ million in 1845, at least one million people died, and, between the period 1845-1850, 1.5 million people emigrated from Ireland.

As early as 17 October 1845, Collins wrote of 'the most alarming accounts of the failure of the staple food of the Irish people'. He predicted that the magnitude of the calamity was such that relief would only be obtained by 'the strenuous exertion of the government supported by the combined efforts of the whole landed proprietary of Ireland'.

In his editorial of 7 November 1845, Collins warned his readers that a severe famine in Ireland was inevitable, and suggested that a partial solution would be for the tenant-farmers to keep their crops of oats, but reported that the majority of the landlords (mainly absentee) were compelling their tenants to sell their grain crops to pay their rents. This editorial also indicates that Collins' thinking was ahead of his time as he promoted measures that modern aid workers are advocating today. He wrote: 'Nothing so retards national development as a habit of looking helplessly to the Ministry in all cases of national difficulty.' He advised that measures should be taken that would enable the people to help themselves.

Collins constantly drew his readers' attention to the dire situation in Ireland, and his descriptive leader articles and campaigning zeal contributed to assisting the starving poor. He berated the eviction of the Irish tenantry, and condemned the law which gave the landlords the right to drive the tenants from their homes like animals. Englishmen, he declared, should not be surprised that Irishmen, thus cruelly and inhumanely treated, turned to the 'wild justice of revenge'.

In April 1846 he criticised the government for the 'revival of the old system of dragooning, imprisoning and transporting the people'. In his editorial of 12 June 1846 he denounced the Coercion Bill, which made thousands of Irish people outcasts, 'heartless and homeless', and confined them to their cabins by a curfew bill, under penalty of transportation for seven years: to a penal colony.

Collins printed letters from Ireland describing in graphic detail the conditions there and these did much to stir the consciences of the people of Hull. One such letter came from Mr. Deane of Skibbereen, an acquaintance of Mr. George Robinson, Manager of the Hull Savings Bank. Mr. Deane wrote that in one parish in his district 14 people had died of hunger in one day, of whom 11 were buried without coffins. He also recorded the overcrowding in the Skibbereen workhouse and explained that people crowded in there to die because they did not want to be interred without coffins.

The *Hull Advertiser* issued on Christmas Day, 1846, carried an editorial by Collins in which he congratulated the Quakers for their many efforts to assist the destitute Irish. He urged the people of Hull to emulate the Subscription Fund set up for Irish Famine Relief by the Society of Friends, and concluded by imploring the people of Hull to do something better for Ireland than 'sneering at her misfortunes, ridiculing her helplessness, and recording her crimes'.

On 20 January 1847 a public meeting took place in the Town Hall, which was attended by representatives from all sectors of society, including 23 clergymen (representing all denominations). A verbatim report of the meeting, which resulted in a Relief Fund being set up, was published in the *Hull Advertiser* on 22 January 1847.

Collins was obviously deeply affected by the enormity of the situation. In his editorial of 29 January 1847 he wrote that the people were daily dying in hundreds, and went on to relate that, in a district of Cork, 5,000 people had perished for want of food, and 25 per cent of the people of the district were already dead. His writing helped to raise public awareness and undoubtedly greatly assisted in the contributions to the Relief Fund. Some of his readers suggested that further funds could be raised by organising bazaars and balls, but Collins was opposed to that idea as he 'disliked the intermingling of the ideas of charity and pleasure'.

Eventually a total of £3,862 was sent to London for despatch to Ireland. A large amount of clothing was also collected and sent to the Society of Friends for distribution through their centres, and was conveyed to London by railway, free of charge.

In February 1847 Collins severely criticised the Mayor and Hull Corporation for being 'indifferent to the alleviation of so much misery' and for refusing to give Hull ratepayers an opportunity to contribute 'a few pence each for the mitigation of a national calamity'. Collins was also critical of some of the Irish Catholic leaders and rebuked Daniel O'Connell for 'poisoning the minds of the Irish people' against the 'Saxon', instead of organising them into 'associations for the advancement of national industry'.

As the potato blight abated, Collins turned his attention to campaigning for the reform of sanitary conditions in Hull. In the autumn of 1847 a group of local doctors formed themselves into a Sanitary Committee and undertook a thorough review of the sanitary conditions in Hull. The secretary of the Committee was Collins' friend, the surgeon, Owen Daly (also a parishioner of St. Charles church). Collins gave the investigation his full support and this, together with his agitations for Poor Law reform, received much publicity in the *Hull Advertiser*. The efforts of Collins and the Hull doctors initially had only a minor effect on the municipal authorities, who made very little attempt to improve Hull's insanitary conditions. The cholera epidemic reached Hull in 1849 and Collins reported that it led to a total of 1,834 deaths or 24.1 per mile, one of the highest rates in the country. At the height of the epidemic the doctors requested a visit from Dr. Sutherland of the General Board of Health, who wrote that, in all his experience, he had never been brought into contact with 'a state of things altogether so abominable or, considering the present state of public health, so dangerous'. Most of the newly arrived immigrants to Hull, particularly the Irish, lived in these insalubrious conditions.

The bulk of the Irish immigrants were Catholics and their religion provoked hostility from the Protestant community. Anti-Catholicism had deep historical roots, stemming from the time of the Reformation, and provided a focus for anti-Irish sentiment. Hull had a long tradition as a Nonconformist town, and there had been periodic anti-Catholic demonstrations. Tickell records that the Catholic Chapel in Posterngate was almost demolished by a fanatical mob in 1780.

In his editorial of 9 July 1847 Collins, in his usual erudite style, condemned a 'No-Popery' campaign during the Beverley elections for 'exacting pledges, from simple-minded electors, not to vote for a Roman Catholic', and advised the 'bigots of Beverley' to stop assuming that they could do 'God's work by standing between Roman Catholics and their enjoyment of rights to which, by the laws of nature and the statute', they were fairly and justly entitled. In the Hull Election campaign in 1847, a 'No-Popery' faction, led by J. R. Pease, was denounced by Collins who said: 'Hatred of any sect of Christians will no longer serve as a common bond of political union.' (*Hull Advertiser*, 11 June 1847).

Stubley, in his recent work on the Evangelicals and the Established Church, wrote that Collins' able defence of Catholics in his newspaper, and on public platforms, helped to prevent prejudice turning into persecution.

Collins had many friends in Hull who supported him in his campaigns for political and social reform. Whenever a controversial (but usually humanitarian) issue was at stake, a cohort of local men rallied to give it their support. The same names appear on memorials, local society lists, subscriptions to good causes, and on documentation in support of Collins. A memorial presented to the Hull Board of Guardians on 14 December 1847, advocating the closure of the workhouse in Whitefriargate, was signed by 38 local men of influence. Their intervention greatly assisted Collins in his campaign for the necessity for a new workhouse in Hull. Throughout the period, Collins used the *Hull Advertiser* as a powerful tool for social reform.

Collins also had his enemies, notably representatives of the shopkeepers and owners of working-class housing, such as Councillor Newton, and Poor Law Guardian, Mr. D. Goodwill, who were only interested in keeping the rates down and objected to improvements in the housing and sanitary conditions in the poorer areas of the city. Collins called these people 'the muck interest' and was unflinching in his condemnation of any local worthies whom he perceived to be unjust or self-seeking. In the *Hull Advertiser* of 1 October 1847 Collins condemned Mr. Goodwill for threatening to publish the names of 'starving recipients of out-door relief' in the newspapers, and pronounced him unfit to fulfil the office of Guardian of the Poor.

Collins was persuasive in his arguments and rebuked all forms of hypocrisy. For example, the Sunday Observance Society and the Evangelicals condemned work on a Sunday. In 1854 the Evangelicals called a meeting to persuade the directors of the Hull and Holderness Railway not to run trains to Withernsea on the Sabbath, but Collins derided these people. In an editorial he pointed out that anyone who employed a groom, coachman or cook on a Sunday was as much a Sabbath breaker as a stoker or guard on a railway train. In his usual pragmatic manner, Collins concluded that, if people went on excursions from Hull on a Sunday, they were at least away from the temptations of the dram and beer shops.

He was an ardent and sincere Catholic and, throughout his journalistic career, lost no opportunity to promote his faith and the Catholic clergy, and to counteract any anti-Catholic opinions expressed nationally or locally. Throughout his time in Hull Collins was very active in the parish life of St. Charles church and frequently referred in his articles to the resident clergy there. He was outspoken on the question of Catholic education, and demanded that Catholics should have the right to have their schools supported out of the taxes, in the same way as any other denomination. (*Hull Advertiser* 10 March 1847).

In the columns of his newspaper he had long intellectual discourses with men of different religious persuasions, and his spirituality and expert knowledge of the scriptures and Catholic dogma are indisputable. It was this aspect of his writing that, in the last few years of his editorship, annoyed the proprietors of the *Hull Advertiser*. They considered that the proper business of a newspaper was to confine itself to the circulation of news, and objected to the prominence that Collins gave to the defensive discussion of the Catholic question. Although chastened, Collins still maintained that Hull, with its frequent 'No-Popery' campaigns, was a place where he had no alternative but to defend his religious convictions and correct the injustices by informing the general public of the falsity of the accusations against Catholics.

There is ample evidence to indicate that Collins did not receive financial security from his years as editor of the *Hull Advertiser*. Collins himself wrote of 'the pecuniary profits of journalism' and, in a lecture given in 1888, William Hunt (an ex-President of the Provincial Newspaper Society) said that Mr. Collins had been 'a brilliant writer, and a most honourable man, but he had lacked the qualities that secured success in business.' In 1848, Collins became the sole proprietor of the *Hull Advertiser*, but, ten years later, the paper was taken over by a limited proprietary company.

Evidence of his changing fortunes is perhaps illustrated by the fact that he frequently moved house. In his evidence, given on 23 June 1853 to the Commissioners who were inquiring into *the Existence of Corrupt Practices in the Borough of Kingston upon Hull,* he told them that he had been a householder since 1847. Collins had therefore been resident in Hull for six years before he owned a property. According to the 1851 Census, his address that year was: 12 Albert Street, Spring Bank. He and his wife had two servants (no children were recorded), and it seemed to be an average middle-class neighbourhood.

The Register of Electors records that, between 1858 and 1860, Collins and his wife lived in Albion Street, which was a much more affluent neighbourhood. However, he was not living there when the 1861 Census was taken. In 1861 and 1862 the Register of Electors records Collins as living in Anlaby Road, and in 1865 at 6 Wilberforce Street, Campbell Street. One can only assume that his house moves coincided with his fluctuations in fortune.

Collins finally retired from the *Hull Advertiser* in 1866 and, in his final address, wrote that 30 years of 'uninterrupted leader article writing is quite sufficient to beget in the mind of a man without political or personal ambition, an exhaustive weariness of such a profession'. He wrote of his failing health and his desire for 'a change of scene'. Appealing for contributions to a testimonial for Mr. Collins' retirement, William Hunt wrote that the ex-editor had worked in a 'noble, unselfish spirit for many years without any adequate temporal reward.' On 22 February 1867 a retirement gift of 400 guineas was presented to him by his friends and colleagues in Hull.

His marriage seems to have been a very happy one as, at that presentation, Collins said that he and his wife had 'lived so happily and been so entirely of one mind'. They retired to London, where he died in January, 1872, at his home: 2, Retreat, Randleshaven Road. The cause of death was certified as 'Morbus Cardis'.

Edward Francis Collins is an enigma. He was bold, uncompromising, tenacious, fearless in confronting opposition, and successful in achieving his aims. Once he was convinced of the validity of a social cause, he pursued it relentlessly and thereby achieved outstanding results. Yet, he was not a success in the dictionary definition of the word, which is given as 'gaining fame, prosperity or status'. Collins gained none of these three rewards.

Hull does not have any record of a physical resemblance of Collins, no painting or statue, nor does he appear in any books of local biographies – although the City now has its Edward Collins Square. He certainly did not gain prosperity, nor did he gain any local status – he was never elected a councillor or magistrate.

However, there is much evidence of Collins: clear insight into the social problems of the day, and his foresight of how these could affect the future. Following a visit to immediate post-Famine Ireland in 1852, he wrote that it was to be deeply regretted that the Irish left their native land carrying with them a 'burning sense of the oppressions heaped upon their race, their country and their creed by England', and saw 'the danger to our children of their bequeathing such legacies of hereditary ill-will to theirs'. This was to be still relevant over a hundred years later,

By today's standards, Collins may have been thought of as sanctimonious, prudish and over-religious, but it was this religious zeal that formed his humanitarian principles and resulted in his great sensitivity towards the under-privileged and socially disadvantaged.

Edward Francis Collins left an indelible mark on the formation of public opinion in Hull, and there is ample evidence to indicate that he was very highly regarded by his contemporaries. The previous owner of the *Hull Advertiser*, Mr. William Bettison, wrote in March 1848 that he had unbounded confidence in Collins' personal and political integrity. Mr. John Leng, of *The Dundee Advertiser*, served his apprenticeship at the *Hull Advertiser*, and recalled that he found Collins to be a kind, considerate and cheerful master, always ready to give advice, encouragement and help. He considered himself fortunate to have joined the press under such an able, scholarly, unselfish and exemplary man,

The editor of the *Eastern Morning News*, William Hunt, wrote (in his publication *Then and Now*) that Collins was a simple-minded, good-hearted man, but 'his sensitive conscience prevented his achieving a success which was easily within the compass of his great abilities'. Hunt went on to say that he had 'the highest respect for Collins whose devotion to opinions sincerely held, earnestness, perseverance, sense of honour and perfection of gentlemanly Christian courtesy, combined with an ever active desire to promote the public good, deserved eminent commendation'.

With accolades and testimonials such as these, it would seem that Hull was very fortunate to have such a man with a sensitive conscience, and willingness and ability to write on the numerous campaigns for local reform. His strong Catholic faith led him to advocate the moral improvement of society. He was also a fervent Radical, promoting free trade, civil and religious liberty, the extension of education, a wider electorate and removal of aristocratic influence. Like Richard Cobden, the eminent politician who died in 1865, he sensed that people and society had to be changed first before the change to Radical politics could take place.

The City of Hull owes much to such an able Victorian campaigner.

Bibliography

Hull Census for 1851.

Report of the Commissioners to inquire into Corrupt Practices in the Borough of Kingston upon Hull, Minutes of Evidence (Ed. Eyre and Wm. Spottiswoode, HMSO 1853).

Hull Advertiser, 1829-1866.

Eastern Morning News, 1865-66.

Carson, R., *The First 100 Years, A History of the Diocese of Middlesbrough 1878-1978* (Middlesbrough, 1978).

Collins, E. F., *Brief Notes of a Short Excursion to Ireland in the Autumn of 1852* (Hull, 1853).

Gillett, E., and MacMahon, K. *History of Hull* (Oxford, 1986).

Gilley, S. and Swift, R., *The Irish in the Victorian City* (Beckenham, 1985).

Hunt, W., *Then and Now: Fifty Years of Newspaper Work* (Hull, 1887).

Sheahan, J. J., *History of Kingston upon Hull*, 2nd edition (Beverley, 1866).

Stubley, P., *A House Divided: Evangelicals and the Establishment in Hull 1770-1914* (Hull, 1995).

Catholicism in nineteenth-century Hull: some perspectives from outside

by

Rev. Dr. Peter Stubley

Whatever their religious affiliation, most English people in the eighteenth and nineteenth centuries, unless they were Roman Catholic, called themselves Protestants. Henry Fielding's lampooning of Mr. Thwackum's opinions was not far from the mark:

> When I mention religion, I mean the Christian religion; and not only the Christian religion, but the Protestant religion; and not only the Protestant religion, but the Church of England.

Catholicism seemed foreign and un-English, especially in Hull under the dominance of Evangelical clergymen, but it was hoped that the monarch's Coronation Oath and the political settlement of 1689 would ensure that Catholicism remained the aberration of a handful of landed gentry and their retainers. Yet in less than a century these cherished bulwarks were no longer proof against Catholic infiltration.

The rising challenge of Catholicism stemmed from the Act of Union in 1800 which merged Ireland with Great Britain, abolished the Irish Parliament and made Westminster directly responsible for Irish affairs. Before the famine of 1840 and the consequent emigration, up to seven million people became the responsibility of the government in London; that five and a half million of them were Roman Catholic inevitably raised fears for the Establishment of the Church of England with its attendant privileges. The population of England and Wales in 1831 was just over fourteen million.

Dissenters wanted equality of status with the Church of England and to see it disestablished, but the Established Church saw Roman Catholics as an even greater threat. They represented an authoritarian, foreign, religio-political power which, given the opportunity, might supplant the Established Church and place a Catholic monarch on England's Protestant throne. The threat was more disturbing since Catholics constituted the large and turbulent majority of the population of Ireland, now part of Great Britain. Through political agitation and religious revival in Ireland and England, Catholics achieved an importance they had not possessed for centuries.

Irish immigrants congregated in London, Liverpool, Birmingham and other large towns where major public works, railways and docks were under construction, but Hull's place on the Eastern seaboard, its links with Protestant Europe, its isolation and characteristic industrial economy, attracted a relatively small number of Irish Catholics.

It might have been supposed that Dissenters and the Church of England in Hull, with their close religious affinities, would join forces against the alleged popish threat, but social and political differences prevented any such alliance. Evangelical Tories suspected Dissenters of radicalism. Ironically, Dissenters and Roman Catholics suffered almost equally from discrimination and were put to similar disadvantage by the exclusive privileges, civil, religious and educational, to which the Established Church clung so tenaciously.

There were church leaders in England who saw the relief of Catholic disabilities as a matter of principle, but the Evangelical clergy in Hull, led by the Rev. John King, vicar of Christ Church from 1822, were vehemently anti-Catholic and fought their cause on every possible occasion. The *Hull Advertiser* went so far as to accuse them of neglecting their pastoral duties for an obsession with religious rectitude and sectarian advantage. While the Rev. Joseph Milner, headmaster of Hull Grammar School (1767-1797), had lamented the worldly distractions of the expanding port, his successors were distracted for half a century by sectarian controversy.

The Relief Act of 1778 permitted Catholic worship. A further Act in 1791 removed restrictions on education and marriage and opened most professions to Catholics. The Emancipation Act of 1829, by allowing Catholics to vote and sit in Parliament, brought them within reach of real political power, and thus of influence over the Established Church. Evangelicals, the Corporation and others in Hull were much alarmed, and protest meetings were held and petitions organised at the time the Bill was going through Parliament.

The clergy sent a petition to both Houses protesting against further concessions of political power to Roman Catholics. Augustus O'Neill, one of Hull's two M.Ps, presented two anti-Catholic petitions in the Commons, one from the Mayor and Aldermen, the other purporting to be signed by 39,000 inhabitants, clergy, bankers, merchants and shipowners. Daniel Sykes, Hull's other M.P., was in favour of Emancipation on grounds of religious liberty, believing that concessions were necessary to prevent civil disorder and danger to the Established Church. He presented a pro-Catholic petition on behalf of Hull Unitarians and 'other friends of religious liberty'. The Church of England's vehement hostility towards Emancipation was tempered by sympathy for the Catholic predicament on the part of a number of Dissenters. Hull's Unitarians were the natural leaders among Dissenters of this frame of mind, a middle-class intelligentsia, marginalised both by the Established Church and by mainstream Nonconformity. Wesleyan Methodists generally, following the example of John Wesley, were unsympathetic towards Catholics. The *Wesleyan Methodist Magazine* saw Emancipation as 'a dangerous encroachment on Church and State by a people given to rebellion'.

Isaac Wilson, editor and proprietor of the *Hull Advertiser*, a Tory with strong anti-Catholic sentiments, proposed a public meeting to make clear the real wishes of 'the thinking inhabitants of Hull.' Wilson was incensed by Sykes' claim that O'Neill's petition had only a few hundred signatures, rather than 3,000 'in all ranks and professions'. The Rev. George Lee, Unitarian editor of the *Hull Rockingham*, backed Sykes and bad feeling developed between the two journals.

The public meeting was held in the Market Place on 2 March 1829, under the shadow of Holy Trinity Church and Peter Scheemaker's equestrian statue of William III, Hull's great symbol of Protestantism. Three hundred were expected, but 5,000 were said to have gathered before

Reverend John Scott I 1772-1834
(By kind permission of the Priest in Charge and Church Wardens, St. Mary the Virgin, Lowgate, Kingston upon Hull).

the meeting began, and this number had swollen to between 8,000 and 10,000 before the end, almost a third of the town's population. The speeches were dominated by the Evangelical clergy, Thomas Dikes of St. John's, John Scott I of St. Mary's, William Knight of St. James', and King. They were in favour of religious freedom, they said, but Roman Catholics could not be trusted with civil power; they were under foreign influence and had no liberty of their own. John King of Christ Church attacked Sykes and asserted that he would now find all Hull against him. This was not true, but King's oratory drew hisses from the crowd every time he mentioned Sykes' name. When, at last, the Rev. Edward Oakes, the Wesleyan minister, was allowed to speak, he took the opportunity to assert Methodism's loyalty to the British constitution.

Once Catholic Emancipation became law, Hull settled down to a period of relative calm with sporadic reports of anti-Catholic feeling. Catholics contrasted the bigotry and intolerance of Tories with the liberality of those in Hull who supported Parliamentary and Municipal Reform in 1832 and 1835. An attempt to obstruct freedom of worship for Catholic workhouse children was one example of the many irritants Catholics had to endure. After the Municipal Corporations Act of 1835, three Catholics were elected to the Town Council and were urged to vote for Reform.

Two men arrived on the scene in 1841 who made important contributions to the Evangelical-Catholic debate; this time not on the side of Evangelicalism. Robert Wilberforce, William Wilberforce's son, was appointed Archdeacon of the East Riding and Rector of Burton Agnes. He came from the parish of East Farleigh in Kent. E. F. Collins, a Roman Catholic and Philosophic Radical came to Hull to edit the *Hull Advertiser*. Wilberforce, much admired by Collins, was a notable example of the off-spring of Evangelical parents who either moved to the Catholic wing of the Church of England or became Roman Catholics. Samuel Wilberforce, Robert's elder brother, was appointed Anglican Bishop of Oxford; John Henry Newman, Henry Manning and Robert Wilberforce, all from Evangelical families, became Roman Catholics. Manning and Newman became cardinals, and Robert Wilberforce died of fever in Rome in 1857 while preparing for the Catholic priesthood.

Robert Wilberforce was a man of his time in his relations with the lower orders. A Tory paternalist with little sympathy for democracy or Dissenting religion, he found the Yorkshire rural clergy uncouth and difficult to handle. This experience and fears about his Catholic sympathies by the more earnest clergy in Hull were a recipe for bad relations and misunderstandings. It was clear where his sympathies lay as soon as he became Archdeacon of the East Riding and rector of Burton Agnes. His own squire accused him of Tractarianism in 1842, and his charge to the clergy the following year, dealing with the Evangelical and Tractarian movements, made it obvious how matters stood. Wilberforce continued to correspond with Newman and Manning; he had known them at Oriel College, Oxford, and he was encouraged to consider the superiority of Catholicism in letters from his ex-curate, William Henn, who had developed Tractarian sympathies with Wilberforce and was received into the Roman Catholic Church in 1850.

The controversy, which led the Archdeacon to secede from the Church of England, began in 1854 over a doctrinal matter, the Eucharist and the Real Presence. It was the subject of Wilberforce's charge to the clergy and he was about to publish a book on the subject. The majority of the Hull clergy took umbrage and signed a letter of protest. They did not have the stomach to take the matter to the ecclesiastical courts, so let things rest once their protest was signed. But the controversy continued to rage week after week in Hull's newspapers, and there was a surprising amount of support for Wilberforce, given the Evangelical ascendency in the Church of England in Hull. Even some who did not sympathise with Wilberforce's views wrote to reprimand the clergy for their constant backbiting; it seemed a largely clerical controversy to Collins and the letter-writers to his newspaper. The typical church-goer at the time was female, middle-class, fashionably dressed and always ready to support her vicar's opinions, 'angels arrayed in Parisian bonnets and Polka jackets.' Wilberforce's position became untenable and he sent his resignation to the Archbishop of York on 30 August 1854 and became a Roman Catholic shortly afterwards. He was about to publish another book, this time on the Royal Supremacy, but could not face another uproar from the Hull clergy.

Collins of the *Advertiser* lamented that the clergy might go on driving people out until no men of learning, piety and zeal were left. The Rev. Thomas Bonnin, curate for the long-time absentee vicar of Sculcoates, observed that the Evangelical clergy were really Dissenters inside the church and would be happier if they joined those outside. The Establishment and their place in an hierarchical society, however, meant so much to Evangelicals that no rapprochement with Dissent was likely.

The restoration of the Catholic hierarchy in England in 1850 provoked a howl of protest from Hull's Evangelical clergy. They demanded a meeting which Robert Wilberforce convened at their request, but he declined to attend himself as an advocate of religious tolerance. Fourteen clergy signed a letter to the Queen requesting her to consider the violation of her supremacy by the Papal Bull which created a new Roman Catholic archiepiscopal see at Westminster. The Archbishop of York, Thomas Musgrove, had no sympathy for Wilberforce's stand and publicly commended those who had signed the address to the Queen.

After 1850 an uneasy feeling was growing in Hull that the Church of England was losing ground against the greater efficiency and zeal of the Church of Rome. This made the visit of Father Alessandro Gavazzi, the ex-Barnabite friar, all the more welcome. He was a friend of Garibaldi, a prolific writer and public speaker who had broken off his allegiance to the papacy. His lecture in Hull's Public Rooms in Jarratt Street in 1856, 'England on the High Road to Popery', sounded just what the Evangelicals wanted, but they were less than pleased when he criticised a proposal to create twelve new Church of England bishoprics which, he said, would be a distraction from real work among the poor. Catholics, he asserted, already did more than the Church of England; because Catholics worked among the poor, so more of the poor became Catholics. His emphasis on the need for working clergy confirmed the fears of those who felt that the Church of England had fallen behind through neglect of the poor, in favour of political controversy and the zeal for purity of doctrine.

In the 1850s and 60s, death removed a generation of old adversaries from the scene. Robert Wilberforce died in 1857. King, the most vehemently out-spoken anti-Catholic in Hull, died in 1858, followed by his lieutenants, Knight in 1862 and Scott in 1865. Anti-Catholic prejudice survived them, of course, but it never again reached the same vituperative heights. Arguably, E. F. Collins' able defence of Catholics in his newspaper and on public platforms helped to prevent prejudice turning into persecution, but he also withdrew from the fray, eventually dying in retirement at Clapham in 1879. He was never a good businessman, and the ownership of the *Advertiser* passed to a limited company in 1851. He continued as editor until 1865 when the paper was incorporated in the *Eastern Morning News*, but in the latter part of his editorship, Collins' attention was given increasingly to non-ecclesiastical affairs, the Dock Company, sanitary reform, the rebuilding of Hull's workhouse, and the establishment of the local board of health. By the 1870s anti-Catholic sentiment in the town had receded almost to the point of indifference, as 'The Great Convent Case' of 1869 suggests.

Protestant mistrust has always been aroused by the 'religious' life of monks and nuns. There had never been a convent in Hull, even in pre-Reformation times. All religious in the town at that period were monks or friars. It was, therefore, something new for Hull when four female novices were received into the Irish Sisterhood of Mercy in St. Charles' church in 1857, to teach in the Catholic girls' schools in Dansom Lane and Canning

Street. The *Hull Packet*, Hull's oldest newspaper, and one of strong Protestant convictions, took great exception to the arrival of these 'prurient brides of Christ'. The *Packet* was upset by the vow to remain unmarried and complained of all the pomp and ceremony at their reception, aimed to impress those of Tractarian sympathies. The Hull Convent Case was extraordinary in that it was not the traditional story, beloved of Protestants, in which a young girl is walled up in a convent against her will. In this case a nun had been expelled from the convent.

Susanna Mary Saurin, an Irish-born nun in the Anlaby Road convent, where the Sisterhood had settled, sued the mother superior for libel and slander and for conspiring to drive her from the order. Sister Mary Scholastica Joseph, as Mary Saurin was known in the order, claimed she had been falsely accused of a series of negligences before an investigating commission, chaired by the Rt. Rev. Robert Cornthwaite, Bishop of Beverley. At the trial, before the Court of the Queen's Bench in Westminster Hall, Sister Mary Joseph, mother superior, referred to as 'Mrs. Star', told how Saurin had been difficult from the time she joined the convent and was recognized by the sisters as the odd one out whom no other order would accept. Her offences were small matters in themselves: eating secretly between meals, borrowing small items from other sisters without their permission, lighting lamps without permission and setting the clock back to cover her lateness for duty. It was alleged that she beat the school children without cause and stole their food. She repeatedly found excuses to talk with externs (people who were not members of the order) and rose early in the morning, again 'without permission', to go into the garden to look for birds' nests.

For these infringements she was eventually demoted from the convent school and set to work in the laundry. She was, said her counsel, obliged to scrub floors, clean the hearth and do every kind of menial work. On one occasion, as a penance, she was forced to wear a dust cloth over her head (she irritated everybody by wearing it longer than required), on another to apologise for lateness by kissing the floor. In her final seven months at Anlaby Road, after refusing to leave the convent of her own accord, she was restricted to a single room, a bed with too few blankets, and condemned to complete silence. Letters were withheld from her and those she wrote were not forwarded. Her food, in the end the leavings of others, was not fit to eat.

The twenty-day trial was packed with spectators, the majority sympathetic to the plaintiff on account of the treatment she had received. Hundreds were unable to get into the court, and the proceedings were fully reported in *The Times* and the Hull newspapers. *The Times* referred to

Mary Saurin as the 'poor lady'. The jury, however, found in favour of the defendants on the counts of assault and imprisonment, and for the plaintiff on the counts of libel and conspiracy, but reduced damages from the £5,000 claimed to £500, including the dowry of £300 which the convent promised to return. It was virtually a victory for the defendants. Saurin withdrew to a convent in Europe as a parlour boarder and the convent in Anlaby Road continued to develop.

Although the case was reported in great detail, anti-Catholic sentiment in 1869 had lost the virulence of 1828-50. Public interest was beginning to wane by the end of the second week, in spite of one leader writer's attempt to keep it going with a salacious revelation of 'a very serious charge of impropriety of conduct', said to be contained in the written statements of the Bishop of Beverley's Commission of Enquiry. It was alleged that Saurin had habitually tried to attract the attention of Father John Motler, assistant at St. Charles' church, and that, becoming greatly excited when he was in the house, she threw herself on her knees beside him and 'asked him to go with her'. Motler was not called to give evidence at the trial and Saurin said she had simply told him on one occasion that lunch was ready.

Comments in Hull were anti-conventual rather than anti-Catholic, ranging from assertions about the 'unnaturalness' of convent life to expressions of satisfaction that the revelations of disorder and uncharitableness proved what people had always suspected. A letter to the editor complained of the suppression of natural affections and that the inmates became tools and chattels of a 'foreign power'. The writer hoped no more convents would be allowed to be built in England, but there was little or no comment apart from that created in the newspapers by themselves. The *Hull Times* said, sneeringly, that although the case merely involved 'women's squabbles' which took up the time of eminent and busy people for almost three weeks, its value lay in the glimpse into convent life, 'which we have long hoped for, but never seen before'. Convents, according to one champion of the Victorian municipal system, should be 'subject to the wholesome and purifying influence of Government inspection'.

The case was soon forgotten; there was little capital to be made from it and interest quickly moved on to other matters, the introduction of Gladstone's Irish Church Bill with its talk of disestablishment and disendowment. A generation was growing up in Hull to whom Roman Catholics, even if still strange and rather foreign, were an acceptable part of the community. The political settlement of 1689 and the threats of 1789, the stuff of life to the Rev. John King and his like, meant nothing to the rising generation. The more recent fears and alarms of 1829 and 1850 were also passing into history.

Another possible reason for the apparent acceptance of Catholicism lay in the town's growing reputation for indifference towards all organised religion. Even Catholics were not immune. A series of articles in 1872 in *The Nation*, an Irish nationalist weekly published in London, entitled 'The Irish in England' by Hugh Heinrick, singled out Hull as the town where the largest proportion of Irish were fallen and lost:

> Hull is the only town I have known where whole families have separated themselves in idea and sentiment from their kindred, and, renegades to Faith and Fatherland, have ranged themselves on the side of England and infidelity. The general condition of the town is low, and the condition of the Irish population corresponds with its surroundings.

Heinrick reckoned the Irish population in Hull to be between 5,000 and 6,000: between 4 and 5 per cent of the total population. In spite of Heinrick's gloomy outlook, at the *Hull News* Religious Census of 1881 there were 2,414 Catholics attending church on census Sunday, 27 November.

The Irish population in Hull may have been 'low' but, for the faithful, an astonishing reminder of the ultramontane triumphalism associated with Cardinal Vaughan's archiepiscopate at Westminster (1892-1903) can still be seen in the interior of St. Charles' church. Many complained of its barn-like baldness when it was opened in 1829, and a number of additions and embellishments were added in 1835. Today's striking and elaborate interior was the work of the local architects Smith, Brodrick and Lowther in 1894. They employed the German artist Heinrich Immenkamp, then living in Hull, who transformed the interior into a highly dramatic version of the lavish late Rococo settings in central and southern Germany. The worshippers at St. Charles' may have been poor in this world's goods and members of a minority religious group in Hull, but such magnificent surroundings spoke the language of a confident internationalism.

Sources
Owen Chadwick, *The Victorian Church* (Black, 1966).
William Hunt, *Hull Newspapers* (Hull, 1880).
David Newsome, *The Parting of Friends* (Murray, 1966).
W. L. Arnstein, *Protestant versus Catholic in Mid-Victorian England* (University of Missouri Press, 1982).
Alan O'Day, *A Survey of the Irish in England in 1872* (Hambledon Press, 1990).
Brian Little, *Catholic Churches Since 1623* (Hull, 1966).
The Victoria History of the County of York East Riding, vol 1 (Oxford University Press, 1969).

Newspapers and Periodicals:

Hull Advertiser	*The Times*
Hull Packet	*Wesleyan Methodist Magazine*
Hull News	*Studies in Church History.*

Mission Impossible? Co-ordination and Catholic Organisations in Hull, 1907-1999

by
Patrick J. Doyle

Would Edward Francis Collins have expressed surprise to witness John Hume M.P., S.D.L.P. Leader, share a platform in Hull Guildhall on 28 January 1999 with a Catholic priest, a Catholic Hull M.P., and a Catholic Leader of the Council? Times have changed from the anti-papal fury in 1850/1 directed against the restoration of the hierarchy, but how much? Prejudice has evaporated, and the small Catholic minority taken its place in civic life in a traditionally Protestant Nonconformist city, but the key may be the very paucity of numbers; estimates of the Catholic population range from 8.1% (1961) to 7% (1990), giving a notional figure of 22,000 nominal Catholics with a weekly Mass attendance of only 4,000.

The immediate post-war decades witnessed a remarkable growth in churches, parishes and schools, followed by a period of decline which saw the closing of St. Vincent's Homes, Endsleigh College of Education, Anchor House, and Kennedy House; the closure of St. Mary's (Wilton Street), St. Patrick's, Saints Peter and Paul; and the reduction of St. Stephen's to a Mass Centre. The experiment of a Bishop in Hull was not repeated, although an Episcopal Vicar has been appointed for Hull and the East Riding. Schools too have closed, namely St. Gregory's, St. Mary's (Wilton Street), St. Bede's, Sacred Heart and St. Wilfrid's, and Marist College amalgamated with St. Mary's High. This paints a bleak picture. However, there is an upside – Endsleigh Pastoral Centre thrives, St. Mary's College is one of the best schools in Hull for academic results, communities of Sisters live on Bransholme and Greatfield Estates, prayer groups flourish, old societies like S.V.P. continue, along with new organisations/approaches like R.C.I.A. and Alpha, while the commitment to the Third World, through Justice and Peace Groups and the Freetown connection, is strong. So all is far from gloom and doom.

This article concentrates upon two themes: first, how Hull has reflected national/international Catholic movements, and, secondly, whether Hull's very isolation and beleaguered state forces the community to become innovators and pioneers. The focus is on three umbrella, inclusive organisations, Federationism, Catholic Action, and the post-Conciliar Pastoral Councils. All three had a presence in Hull.

Federationism, the brainchild of Bishop Casartelli of Salford, was based on German models of lay/clerical cooperation and co-ordination. Federations were simple yet complex organisations; they were free-standing associations which also tried to co-ordinate the work of other, older Catholic groups with their own allegiances, and Casartelli tried to form a Confederation bringing together on a national scale all local Federations. At one level Federations were innovative, but at heart they were defensive, their culture based on reactions to Bismarck's *Kulturkampf* and the French anti-clerical laws, which saw *inter alia* the Canonesses of St. Augustine establish their school, 'the French Convent', in Park Grove. Alongside the Federation was a longer-lasting development, the National Catholic Congresses. The first was held at Leeds in 1910.

In Hull, Father Thomas Wright, curate at St. Mary's (Wilton Street), founded the Hull Federation in 1907 with the help of laymen such as A. Dowling, R. Galloway and J. O'Hara. Each parish was invited to send delegates to a Central Executive, which met at 81 Charles Street. They operated at various levels, and had initial successes with a series of lectures at the Royal Institution. Speakers included Hilaire Belloc, Mgr. R. H. Benson, Bishop Keating of Northampton (later Liverpool), and the Editor of *The Universe*, G. E. Anstruther. In 1909, 2,000 people attended a meeting addressed by Dr. Francis Bourne, Cardinal Archbishop of Westminster. These rallies served many purposes, raising the morale of an isolated small Catholic body, and provided a public programme for anyone interested in Catholicism, an indirect form of evangelisation.

One-off big events are time-consuming, but relatively easy to organise. Likewise, defensive reactions rally people to the cause, so there was a flurry of activity around the protection of Catholic pauper and delinquent children in institutional care, and Catholic rights in the new cemetery. Other basic work included electoral registration (before 1918 it was not always easy to register for a vote), and the promotion of Catholic social teaching. A debating society, a savings club, and a Catholic employment scheme were formed. Evening classes in commercial subjects were provided for Catholic boys denied a secondary education (Marist College was not founded until 1925). A 'heady' programme, but, as ever, one wonders whether the euphoria of reports and minutes reflected reality. The Federation's weaknesses were exposed in many ways – for instance, the Liberal Government's plans for a National Insurance Scheme, in which

Friendly Societies played a central role, demonstrated a fundamental Catholic weakness. There was no single Catholic Friendly Society; yet, from the Church's perspective, the scheme provided Catholic visitors who could keep the 'lax and lapsed' within the orbit of the Church. The Salford Federation in 1912 argued for a national organisation, but in Hull there were three different bodies. The Catholic Benefit Society had its registered office on Spring Bank West, and its Pope Leo XIII branch at St. Charles, which claimed to offer better benefits than the Oddfellows and Foresters. The Irish Ancient Order of Hibernians was based at St. Mary's (Wilton Street), while St. Vincent's had a branch of the National Catholic Thrift Society . . . so much for co-ordination.

But the real divisions were political. The Irish were committed to Home Rule, while other Catholics gave priority to their denominational schools. Thomas F. Burns, Bishop Casartelli's lay adviser, introduced another dimension: he was anti-Labour and obsessed with the creation of a Catholic political party. During the Hull municipal elections in 1910, the removal of R. Galloway (the Catholic representative) from the Education Committee), and the status of St. Mary's (Girls) Grammar School were issues. The actions of the Liberal controlled Council were opposed by both the Federation and the Irish, but in West Central Ward, the Nationalist's Chairman, J. McLaughlin, supported the Liberal, W. L. Harrison, against the Conservative, F. Hare, who was backed by Federationists like J. O'Hara. In 1911 the Nationalists' secretary, J. O'Hara, fought Paragon, which covered the Irish West End, but lost by 58; and in the following year he lost again to Councillor Wheatley, who received support from Catholics like Mr. Thomas F. Farrell because of his defence of Catholic schools. Not surprisingly, during a bitterly contested West Hull parliamentary by-election in 1907, the divisions in Catholic ranks were threefold. The Federation backed the Unionist, Sir George Bartley, the leading Nationalists backed the successful Liberal, Guy Wilson, and some Irish urged their fellow countrymen to vote for James Holmes, the Labour candidate, if they felt he could win.

How strong was the Irish vote? In 1881 there were 2,474 Irish-born in the town. Hull was not Liverpool or Glasgow; their numbers were too small even to win Paragon. This was partly because of the substantial business roll in the centre, as well as under-registration of votes. However, despite small numbers the Hull Irish were well organised, and during the heyday of the Home Rule agitation, 1908-11, Nationalist Members of Parliament, J. C. Flynn, D. Sheehy, J. P. Farrell and P. J. Brady, spoke at Hull St. Patrick's Day rallies. Brady and the United Irish League Yorkshire Organiser, T. Shennan, in the 1911 Central Hull by-election shared the platform with the Liberal candidate, Robert Aske, against the Catholic Conservative, Mark Sykes of Sledmere. Home Rule drove the Irish into the Liberal camp. McLaughlin, O'Hara, Coonan and others signed Aske's nomination papers, but for how long could this alliance last? Amidst the turmoil more pointers appeared: during the 1911 strikes Dean Hall took collections for the distressed families of strikers, and, when the strike fever swept through schools across the country, the boys of St. Charles were at the forefront of the Hull Schools' Strike, even sending a flying picket to Wilton Street.

Meanwhile, some Hull Federationists and priests played a part in the national scene. Dean Hall of St. Charles and M. Regan attended the Leeds Congress in 1910, as representatives of the Diocese, Fr. Wright addressed a section meeting on the attitudes of Federations to elections, and J. O'Hara presented a paper on the combining of Federations. At the Newcastle Congress in 1911 Fr. Wright spoke on the Catholic Press. In 1909 amendments were moved by Hull Federationists at a Confederation meeting in London, and J. Boland became Vice Chairman, while T. Kennedy became a committee member of the Catholic Trades Unionist Association, an offshoot of the Confederation. Links remained with the Congresses. For instance, Lady Sykes spoke on 'Women in national and international affairs' at the 1926 Manchester Congress, but by then they were triennial, and the last was convened in 1929 (ironically the centenary of Catholic Emancipation). Federationism in Hull did not survive Father Wright's leaving Wilton Street in 1912, which raises questions about the sustainability of his initiatives. How strong are organisations which depend on the energies of one person?

To return to the political Irish, the 207 names on the St. Charles Roll of Honour for the 1914-18 War are predominantly Irish, and are indicative of assimilation. The 1916 Easter Rising and the eventual establishment of the Irish Free State had far-reaching consequences. Hull had its own connections with the Troubles, not least the presence at Endsleigh of Sister Mary Celestine (Michael Collins' sister, Helena), and in Commander Kenworthy (Liberal M.P. for Hull Central), a leading member of the Peace with Ireland Council, a strong supporter of Irish Independence. He spoke in the Commons against the Black and Tans, and in favour of the Sinn Fein hunger strikers in Wormwood Scrubs. In 1920 he explained that the strong support on Hull docks for the Irish was the reason for industrial unrest in the port. The sudden death of Arthur Griffith and the slaying of Michael Collins in 1922 saw the largest and last Irish demonstration in Hull, when a huge parade processed from Pryme Street to St. Patrick's for a Requiem Mass for the two dead leaders. It was a muted affair, not least because of the bitter Irish Civil War and the shock of the young leader's violent death. In 1926 Kenworthy significantly left the Liberal Party and joined Labour. With characteristic honesty he resigned, then fought and won the subsequent by-election.

On the whole the Irish followed the M.P. into Labour's camp. Despite Thomas Burns and Casartelli's attempts to have Labour condemned as an atheistic quasi-communist party, the wiser counsels of Archbishops Bourne and Keating prevailed. A new era emerged, with bulldozers moving into the slums of Mill Street, and with the building of Ferensway the Irish were dispersed, many into North Hull, and assimilated (after the creation of the Irish Free State) into local politics. They were overwhelmingly working class. Labour was their party. Interestingly, the General Election of 1997 produced 60 Catholic Members of Parliament, of whom 42 were Labour (45 including their SDLP allies). The House of Lords presents a very different picture – 85 Catholics, only seven Labour (including three Life Peers created in 1997).

The Catholic Church faced new threats in the Twenties and Thirties, on the world stage those of Communism and Fascism, and at home, despite the growth in numbers (which included a crop of notable converts, among them the novelists Graham Greene and Evelyn Waugh), there were signs of what was termed 'leakage' or 'lapsing'. New approaches were required, and Catholic Action emerged on the Continent. Some Hull people immersed themselves in these new movements. In the late Canon Clifford's library were two significant books: *Restoring all things: a guide to Catholic Action* (1939) and Philip Hughes' *The Pope's New Order: a systematic summary of the Social Encyclicals and Addresses* (1943). Among his surviving papers are a summary of lecture notes dated November 1938, with Catholic Action defined as *'the participation of the laity in the apostolate of the Church's Hierarchy'.*

War has been perceived by many historians as an agent of social change; so, rather than disappearing with the advent of the Second World War, the conflict proved a stimulus to Catholic Action. In Hull R. A. Twomey proved a pivotal figure; along with W. G. Nevin he was attending Diocesan Catholic Action Council meetings in 1940. In the following year Hull Catholic Action produced a threefold programme: (1) prayers for peace, (2) the study of Pius XII's *Summi Pontificatus*, and post-war reconstruction, and (3) action to assist the poor and the evacuees, help with billeting, and the formation of Young Christian Worker branches.

On the national scene the Yorkshire-born Cardinal Hinsley of Westminster, with other Church leaders, signed a famous letter to *The Times* in 1940, which outlined principles for post-war renewal, including the abolition of extreme inequalities, the safeguarding of the family, and prophetically arguing that the *'resources of the earth should be used as God's gift for the whole human race, and generations yet to live'*. Arising from this initiative the Cardinal, along with lay people such as Christopher Dawson, Barbara Ward, and A. C. F. Beales, formed the 'Sword of the Spirit', issuing a flood of pamphlets, organising study groups and rallies, and encouraging non-Catholic membership. Unbelievably, even in those pre-ecumenical times Hinsley's decision to say the Lord's Prayer with other Christians at a rally in 1941 led to the active hostility of other bishops. The Sword became a Catholic-only movement, and others had to form their own Religion and Life movement. Hinsley's death in 1943 reduced the Sword's influence, but it continued. The 1945 Hull Catholic Action Report referred to monthly meetings, which focused on practical problems (with Miss D. M. Drewery the contact). In 1946 the Sword held a summer school at Marist College, with Fr. Paul Crane S.J. speaking on Social Justice.

In 1945 the local committee, to give its full title 'The Hull Joint Committee of Clergy and Catholic Action', organised a Catholic Week, from 28 May to 3 June at Endsleigh College. Each night there was a main speaker on important themes, i.e. 'Should Youth Serve or be Served?' by Baroness Bosche van Drakestein; 'When the Boys and Girls Come Home' by the Principal R.A.F. Chaplain, Mgr. Beauchamp; 'Some Notes on Catholic History', by the Principal of Endsleigh, Mother Mary of God; 'The Family', by Father Agnellus Andrew O.F.M.; and on 'The Catholic Contribution to Post War Reconstruction' by Sir Patrick Hannon, M.P. On Sunday, 3 June, a Solemn High Mass was celebrated at St. Charles, with a rally at the Tivoli Theatre, which featured the Archbishop of Westminster, Bernard Griffin, on 'Christian Responsibility', and the Sword of Spirit stalwart, Barbara Ward, on 'The Basis of a Constructive Peace'. The Lord Mayor, Councillor Nicholson, held a civic reception in honour of the Archbishop.

How was the Committee constituted? Like the Federation, each Parish Priest was a member, plus a parishioner appointed by him, and every organisation (such as the Catenians, Knights of St. Columba, Catholic Doctors' Guild, the Apostleship of the Sea, the Union of Catholic Mothers, the Catholic Women's League, and the S.V.P.) all provided one representative. There were powers to co-opt. The 1945 report indicated that new groups were fostered, like the Legion of Catholic Serving and ex-Servicemen, which helped the demobbed; Mrs. Bates found lodgings for some 50 Catholic visitors to the city; hospitality was given to Dutch children, with the C.W.L. providing tea parties; the Apostleship of the Sea used Charles Street and received 4,000 seafarers and servicemen; Mr.

T. Geraghty of the *Hull Daily Mail* worked on vocational guidance; and in 1946 mention was made of a Catholic Debating Society, whose secretary, Miss Q. Dunne (as Councillor Helen Wilson) later chaired the City Council's Cultural Services Committee.

Were the Catholic Weeks repeated? Yes, in 1948 there were plans for another series of talks, including Father Agnellus O.F.M. again, A. C. F. Beales, T. Leyland of the Catholic Social Guild, the Archbishop of Birmingham, and Mr. Foley (presumably Maurice Foley, later a Labour M.P. and Junior Minister?). Did the aims remain the same? In 1949 they were listed as 'defend the Faith', 'promote the Faith', and 'study the Social Problem'. Was there an ecumenical dimension? Representatives served on the Hull Standing Conference of Youth, the British Council (re Foreign Sessions), the Council of Christians and Jews, the Hull Council for Old People's Welfare, and the Federation of Girls and Mixed Clubs. Interestingly, the A.G.M. of the Apostleship of the Sea was held in the City Council Chamber and is it of significance that two of the 1949 Public Representation Committee of 1949, Harold Ashton and Jimmy Mullaney, became councillors?

The Schools campaign deserves special mention; plans were drawn up in 1949 in a belated response to the 1944 Education Act. A memo indicated that the Catholic contribution towards alterations, rebuilding and new provision would amount to £220,917. Eight primaries were planned: at St. Charles, St. Gregory's, St. Mary's (Wilton Street), St. Vincent's, Sacred Heart, Endsleigh, St. Wilfrid's, and Holy Name (of these only four survive) to cater for 1,870 pupils. Two Grammar Schools – Marist and St. Mary's – were to provide 660 places, with three new modern schools, Boys, Girls, and mixed, for 1,350 children – a grand total of 3,750.

With the approach of a General Election, a Hull case was prepared, and copies of the Catholic Parents and Electors Association memorandum, and leaflets issued by the *Stella Maris* magazine were acquired. All candidates for Labour, Conservative and Liberal parties in the four constituencies of Hull East, North and West, plus Haltemprice, were lobbied, some in person, others by telephone, or by questionnaire and letters. The exercise was not very useful – few candidates wishing to win a seat willingly alienate a sizeable proportion of their electorate. However, it did remind all parties of Catholic strength, and the Church's ability to mobilise, as and when required. Nonetheless, 'all age' schools persisted in Hull well into the Sixties, until eventually St. Richard's, St. John Fisher and St. Thomas More were opened as the 'modern schools'. Before long they became Junior High Schools, following comprehensive re-organisation.

Was the Schools' lobby the high water of Catholic Action in Hull? Soon after, the movement seemed to decline, though it left a legacy. The Y.C.W. survived in some parishes into the Seventies, Anchor House was built, the Catholic Local History Society flourished, and the Catholic Social Guild continued with Frances and Charles Brady as prominent members – both later councillors. The Sword of the Spirit, in effect, became the Catholic Institute for International Relations, and CAFOD was another offspring, so the present Justice and Peace groups can trace their lineage back to the Sword, and the Forties.

Like the Federation, does the surviving documentation exaggerate the strength of Catholic Action? Even in 1949 a rail excursion to Walsingham had to be cancelled, as only 80 people had signed up, and in December of that year the minutes plaintively recorded, *'We have a large Council membership and most of our members apparently find it difficult to do more.'* How much depended upon the likes of Mr. Twomey? Do most organisations eventually run out of steam unless renewed? Renewal was near, but few in the Fifties could have anticipated the hurricane of Vatican II. Yet there were stirrings abroad. Fr. Clifford Howell's writings on the liturgy produced the 'dialogue Mass', Pius XII introduced the reforms of the Holy Week services, and there was the work of pastoral Centres such as Spode House, the Grail, and Y.C.W. – the latter's 'See, Judge and Act' methodology became the post-Conciliar 'pastoral cycle'. Also individual theologians and writers reflected Continental trends and prepared the younger generation, and the young at heart, for Pope John XXIII.

The latest attempt to develop an over-arching organisation emerged in 1981 with the arrival in Hull of Bishop Kevin O'Brien, former Vicar General of Leeds and President of the Catholic Missionary Society. The auxiliary's Pastoral Council reflected the emphasis upon lay involvement and collaborative ministry of the Second Vatican Council. The Decree on the Apostolate of the Laity made specific reference to establishing national congresses and pastoral councils at diocesan, deanery and parish levels. Unfortunately, the decree added the weasel words *'where possible'*. A national Pastoral Council was held in Liverpool, but was a 'one off' – so, despite the Council, there is no equivalent of the Church of England Synods and Assemblies, or the Methodist Conferences. Instead, there is a patchwork quilt of local initiatives, among which there remains the Hull and District Pastoral Council. Ironically, there were National Conferences in England and Wales between 1910 and 1929. The Federations and Catholic Action Joint Committees provided a history of joined-up working without any Conciliar decree, which makes the lack of overall contemporary organisations quite extraordinary.

The Pastoral Council covers the two Deaneries, which split the city in two, and like its predecessors is supposed to have representatives from every parish and society, and effective liaison with the priests of the Deaneries. Inevitably it is 'top down', and often perceived as just another group or society, and certainly not as the co-ordinating body. Recently the Pastoral Council has applied to itself the test of the very Catholic principle of subsidiarity – that is, it should only perform those tasks which individual parishes cannot undertake. In other words, it should co-ordinate, enable, and sponsor, as well as organise.

Perhaps Hull 700 is an ideal opportunity, with the perspective of the Federation and Catholic Action, to re-examine the strengths and weaknesses of their successor – although this writer might be too close to the Pastoral Council to be completely objective. But how many other Deaneries staged a series of lectures to commemorate *Rerum Novarum's* Centenary in 1991, when Pope John Paul II specifically asked for his encyclical, *Centesimus Annus* to be studied by the laity? How many cities in the wake of the Bishops' pre-election statement, 'The Common Good', organised a public meeting? A packed ecumenical audience at Endsleigh heard the views of, and debated with, Kevin McNamara, M.P. (Labour, Hull North) and Edward Leigh, M.P. (Conservative, Gainsborough). How many have staged annual Pastoral Assemblies on the themes of 'Son, Holy Spirit and The Father' in preparation for the Millennium, in response to the Pope's encyclical, *'Adventio Tertio Millennio'*? Clearly these are Deanery-wide matters, but the obvious weakness is the failure to engage with the parishes. Where is the preparation, follow-up and feedback? The Pastoral Council has undertaken the responsibility for the Catholic contribution to Hull 700, and the City's (not the diocese's) commemoration of the Millennium. This argues the value of a permanent body, rather than having to set up *ad hoc* bodies. What are the other successes? The 'Drop In' at St. Charles Centre (81 Charles Street), held every Tuesday morning helps the City-centre homeless, as well as providing a meeting place for Catholics from every parish. The Endsleigh Discussion Forum meeting every second Sunday in the month fills the gap left by the demise of the Newman Association, talks on Scripture have proved popular, and the mornings for Eucharistic Ministers are always well attended. In terms of sponsorship the Council has collaborated with the ecumenical Rerum Novarum Group, encouraged the formation of Credit Unions, and continued to foster the Hull-Freetown (Sierra Leone) link. It is a uniquely Hull institution. There are no constitutional links with any national or, indeed, diocesan organisations, and there are no Pastoral Council delegates on any other body. It has been a struggle to fill the East Hull places on the executive –

everything is accomplished on a 'wing and a prayer' with slender resources, but it has kept going. Hull's very isolation and the small Catholic population have made the City find its own solutions. Also, even if small in numbers their achievements are considerable in a place with the lowest church attendance in the country.

What conclusions can be drawn? Without due recognition and support, all such groups will wither. There is a danger in a 'top down' structure of initial success leading to long-term failure, because of the absence of 'ownership'. Key personnel such as Fr. Wright and R. A. Twomey are hard to replace, and persistence is required. Should the work of the Pastoral Council ever blossom, then it could not rely upon unpaid volunteers to provide the secretariat. What are the future challenges? If the Pastoral Council survives, will it develop ecumenical links with similar bodies? Will it have delegates on the Inter-Faith Forum? Will it engage with CityVision and the regeneration agenda? Will parishes respond to the new Council structures of Area and Ward Forums? Let the historians of Hull 800 ponder and hopefully provide the answers. Meanwhile, in contemporary Hull we have to wrestle with the problem of how to create a flexible, sustainable organisation.

Bibliography
Adrian Hastings, *A History of English Christianity, 1920-1985* (1986).
J. M. Cleary, *Catholic Social Action in Britain, 1909-1959: A History of the Catholic Social Guild* (1961).
Robert Carson, *The First 100 Years, A History of the Diocese of Middlesbrough, 1878-1978* (Middlesbrough, 1978).
Patrick J. Doyle, 'Religion, Politics and the Catholic Working Class', *New Blackfriars* (May, 1973).
Patrick J. Doyle, 'The Church's Option in Hull', *New Blackfriars* (February, 1988).
Patrick J. Doyle, 'Mission – Where Possible', *New Blackfriars* (April, 1995).
Patrick J. Doyle, 'Accommodation or Confrontation: Catholic Response to the Formation of the Labour Party', *(North West Labour History*, No. 16, 1991/2).
Two files rescued from the old St. Patrick's Presbytery, relating to 'Catholic Action in Hull' in the possession of the author.

Catholics in Hull Public Life

by
John Markham

'Let us now praise famous men,' urges the Book of Ecclesiasticus, but, after listing those who deserve great honour, continues with the reminder, 'Some there be who leave no memorial'. These are the people who lead good lives and are equally deserving of praise.

Among the vast army of anonymous saints are many local Catholics whose righteousness has not been commemorated with any statue or street name. Inevitably, with the passing of time, memories fade of men and women who were once shining lights within their own circles of family, friends and colleagues.

Arthur Birtles

Arthur Birtles, for example, spent his entire teaching career, 1911-50, at Hymers College, for much of this time as the senior history master. Boys, unaware of his real Christian name, knew him as 'Alfie', and his mannerisms and his repeated sayings – *'Toujours la politesse'* was one – ensured that he was imitated more than any other member of staff. Yet, camouflaged by contagious ridicule was great admiration and affection for a man who had a profound effect on many lives, developing a love of history, guiding them through to university places and, even more fundamentally, illustrating through his kindness and his courteous example his own moral code and spiritual values.

Outside school he led a simple celibate life. His address, 59 De Grey Street, was more modest than his colleagues considered fitting for a master at Hymers, he rode hazardously through Hull on an old bicycle, and it was reputed that, when he allowed himself the luxury of a visit to the New Theatre, he paid the minimum price, which allowed him to stand at the back. He gave a large part of his income away, was a member of one of the minor religious orders, and, as a most devout parishioner of St. Vincent's church, never passed it without going inside and following the Stations of the Cross, often so short of time on his way to school that it was done at the speed of an express train.

He was a great admirer of the first headmaster of Hymers, C. H. Gore, who had appointed him as a young, inexperienced graduate with a Leeds M.A. Gore was another gentlemanly, courteous man, a total contrast to his successor, W. V. Cavill, who ran a harsh régime, at times of indefensible severity. 'Alfie' Birtles himself never punished, relying solely on words to bring about reformation, and his right to be regarded as a modern saint is surely strengthened by the crisis of conscience he must have weathered in maintaining his complete loyalty to a headmaster of very different character who made no secret of his anti-Catholic views.

Praised by HMIs for his 'quite outstanding work', he would have had no difficulty in a later period in securing a senior post in higher education, but he found fulfilment in his vocation and did not complain. The circumstances of his unexpectedly early retirement through illness robbed him of the tributes normally paid to a long-serving teacher. The others whose careers are discussed in this chapter all enjoyed more public recognition of their success, though this is an appropriate time to recall aspects of their lives which should not be allowed to pass into oblivion.

Bibliography
F. W. Scott, A. Sutton, N. J. King, *Hymers College – The First Hundred Years* (Beverley, 1992).

Very Rev. Dean Michael Trappes, 1797-1873

It is only to be expected if a priest is prominent within his parish, but there is one who stands out as a well-known member of the wider Hull community in the 19th century: Michael Trappes, who came to St. Charles church in 1848 and remained there for the rest of his life.

He was born in the North Riding in 1797, studied at Ushaw, and had a varied experience of pastoral work in the North of England before taking up his post at Hull, where he quickly established himself as a man of considerable influence. In her publication, *The Catholic Revival in Yorkshire 1850-1900*, Jennifer V. Supple-Green describes Trappes as a priest 'reared in the old atmosphere of clerical independence' but one who progressed from championing the rights of the clergy in the 1850s to being 'welcomed as an adviser not only to his fellow priests but also to his bishop'.

In addition to working in the cause of education in Hull he took a full part in Catholic charities, but it was his extra-mural work which, as she says, helped to make Catholics acceptable and respectable, and, with a few exceptions, respected by the Protestants, who were so strong in Hull. Unlike those priests who – even at a much later date – tended to look inwardly to their own parishioners, he had no hesitation in participating in the public life of the town, joining the Hull Literary and Philosophical Society and lecturing at the Mechanics Institute.

There were, of course, some who did not approve. In 1859 Robert Hardey, a surgeon of a strongly Protestant persuasion, attacked the Liberal M.P., James Clay, for not being a Protestant: his evidence was that Clay had been seen in the streets of Hull walking arm in arm with Father Michael Trappes. Clay's own religious views are not easily identifiable, but he was a man of tolerant outlook, critical of sectarian myopia, and he replied that, although the incident had happened nine or ten years previously and he would be unable to recognise Father Trappes if he met him, if he did so he would not have the slightest objection to walking down the street with him, or indeed with 'any other Catholics of equally estimable character and accomplishments'. The fact that Mr. Hardey was in a distinct minority was borne out by the sound of 'much cheering and support' which greeted Clay's reply.

An illustration of Trappes' determination that Catholics should see themselves as full members of the national community occurs in Sheahan's reference to the marriage of the Prince and Princess of Wales (later Edward VII and Queen Alexandra) in 1863. Apart from the special service at Holy Trinity, he points out there was only one other of its kind held in Hull, This was at St. Charles, where 200 children from Catholic schools processed to the church and, as they entered, the National Anthem was sung 'with great spirit, one of the priests acting as conductor. During the service Trappes 'strongly impressed upon his hearers the duty of praying fervently for the welfare of the royal couple'. No longer were Catholics a people set apart.

Dean Trappes did not neglect his prime duties as a priest. By the 1860s he was anxious to improve the welfare of the poor dwellers in the district known as the West End 'and to bring God's house nearer to those who, through poverty and misfortune, often stayed away from Holy Mass and neglected to send their children to school'. With his colleagues, Frs. Arthur Riddell (later Bishop of Northampton) and John Motler, he began a weekly outdoor collection to raise funds to erect a church and school in Mill Street, the very centre of this densely populated Irish area. A site was secured, Edward Simpson, a Catholic architect, was commissioned to prepare plans, and building began in the spring of 1871, with the laying of the foundation stone fixed for St. Patrick's Day that year.

Processions and public ceremonies of any kind were always sure of a good audience in Hull, and this was no exception: 'About noon of that auspicious day crowds began to assemble around the site of the proposed new Chapel, and, as the procession of the Clergy and attendants came in view, a shout of joy arose from the assembled throng'. There was, however, great disappointment that Dean Trappes was indisposed and unable to join the celebrations on this great day, but the Very Rev. Canon Motler, now from Bradford, performed the stone-laying ceremony on Dean Trappes' behalf. The formal opening of the chapel came quickly after, on 7 November, with the Bishop of Beverley, Dr. Robert Cornthwaite, present at High Mass, which was followed by a luncheon at the Royal Station Hotel.

In recognition of his achievements, a number of Catholic gentlemen had presented Trappes with 100 sovereigns in 1861 as a 'slight token of the great service which he had rendered to the Catholic cause during the 13 years that he has been amongst them'.

The Very Rev. Dean Trappes died at St. Charles' Presbytery in 1873, aged 76. 'There was no priest,' wrote Edmund Wrigglesworth over 30 years later, 'whose memory is held in greater veneration by the Catholics of Hull', and he quoted from the funeral oration preached by Canon Consitt, which described Dean Trappes as 'open of hand and open of heart, genial and true, the mirror of honour and truthfulness, scorning everything mean and shabby, frank and outspoken, a faithful friend and a courteous gentleman, without fear and without reproach – a true priest of God'.

Bibliography

J. F. Supple-Green, *The Catholic Revival in Yorkshire 1850-1900* (The Leeds Philosophical and Literary Society, 1990).

E. Wrigglesworth, 'The Parish of St. Patrick, Hull', in *Souvenir of Killarney in Hull* (programme for a three-day bazaar) (Hull, 1905).

J. Markham, *Disraeli's Fellow Traveller – James Clay, M.P. for Hull.* (Beverley, 1997).

Andrew McManus, 1798-1866

Andrew McManus was Hull's first Chief Constable and a man of great influence in the town for 30 years.

Apparently little is known of his early life, although A. A. Clarke, the historian of the Hull Police Force, points out that he had been a member of the Connaught Rangers and, when he later held his important post in Hull, he was happy to let leading citizens hold the erroneous belief that he had previously been a commissioned officer in the army.

An obituary notice, summarising his distinguished career, stated that, while he was being trained at the London Constabulary School, his ability was noted and he was appointed Inspector of Kensington Palace when it was the home of Queen Victoria's mother, the Duchess of Kent. Likely promotion in London was overtaken by his appointment as superintendent of the newly formed Hull police force in 1836, and the impression he made was so great that his initial salary of £150 p.a. was upgraded to £200 long before the trial six-month period was complete. In 1839 he was given the title of Chief Constable.

Tributes to his ability and his achievements are too frequent and consistent to be dismissed as flattery. He was, everyone agrees, a most efficient organiser, a strict disciplinarian who nevertheless gave praise when praise was due, he 'abhorred every form of espionage save that of watching an individual liable to arrest on some criminal charge', and he was also courteous, intelligent and quick to discern the gradations of rank, so as to be observant and respectful without being obtrusive'. In the interests of historical accuracy, it has to be noted that Mr. Clarke quotes one critic who described him as a 'plethoric, choleric', red-faced man, whose size reflected his love of food and drink.

To McManus goes the credit for establishing an excellent fire brigade, then part of the police force, and, even more importantly, ensuring that Hull earned a reputation for having 'the most efficient police force in the Kingdom'.

He had been in poor health for some time when the death of his wife in January 1866 aggravated his problems, and he died in April that year at the house of his surgeon son in Withernsea. His body was brought by train to Southcoates Station and taken to St. Charles for the burial service. Chief Constable McManus had served Hull for 30 years, and, as the one who had moulded and guided it through its critical early period, he fully deserves his honoured place in the annals of Hull police history.

Bibliography
A. A. Clarke. *The Policemen of Hull* (Cherry Burton, 1992).
Obituaries in *Hull Advertiser* and *Hull Morning News*.

Joseph James Sheahan, 1814-93

Joseph James Sheahan established his reputation by the publication in 1864 of the *History of the Town and People of Kingston-Upon-Hull*, a work far more accessible than the older histories of the town by such authors as Hadley and Tickell, and particularly valuable for its detailed accounts of

19th-century institutions, buildings and events: he had the sense to realise that the happenings of his own lifetime would one day be history.

His career is further proof that, whatever the obstacles placed in their way by prejudice, Catholics of ability were able to make their mark. Although he was said to have received a good education, his formal studies probably ended at an early age and his extensive knowledge of history, not merely that of Hull, came through his own application and discoveries.

Sheahan was born in Cork in 1814, and, after a relatively unsuccessful venture on the stage in Ireland, moved to London and then to the North of England, where he joined Ira Aldridge, 'the African Roscius', for five years, all the while pursuing his study of history. It was during a tour with Aldridge that he first encountered Hull, in 1841 when he was 27. What decided him to give up his wanderings and settle is unknown, but perhaps he saw it as an interesting place with a developing story which needed recording for a growing number of potentially interested readers. In any event, he made his home in Hull, took a post with a firm of sharebrokers in Bowlalley Lane, which he found uncongenial, and continued to enlarge his historical knowledge. As early as 1848 he had begun to compile his *magnum opus* which no doubt provided welcome relief from his less interesting occupation.

About this time he moved to Tiger Lane, Beverley, and the *Status Animarum* prepared by Father Henry Walker for St. John's church in 1855 shows him living there with his wife and four children, fulfilling their religious duties of confirmation, communion and confession. Mrs. Sheahan was the daughter of Job Marson, who lived in the same lane, and who was shown in the *Status Animarum* as having an equally staunch Catholic family. Marson was a trainer, renowned for training Nancy, winner of the Chester Cup and the Goodwood Cup in 1851, and the father of a celebrated jockey of the same name.

The history which Sheahan compiled remained the standard work for many years and is still a most useful source of information on aspects of 19th-century history not recorded elsewhere. By modern publishing standards it is a formidable volume of around 800 closely packed pages of small print. It is proof, too, of his enormous industry, so typical of the Victorians, with its careful compilation of facts and figures, the dimensions of buildings, and the names of people present at events: a book of a type which will never again be published. Yet, although it lacks the thematic approach and the analysis which would be expected of a modern historian, it is still a readable book, and, while its concise style allows considerable information to be packed within a short space, there are more subtle and indirect comments and judgements than appear at a casual reading.

He was admirably fair to Protestants and Jews, and wrote without bias on their history and their buildings. While not intruding his own personality, he revealed that he had been present at an open-air meeting addressed by James Clay, the Liberal M.P. and an outstanding orator who could be heard distinctly on the further extremity of a crowd of at least 10,000. Using the editorial first-person plural, he added: 'we have heard many excellent open-air speakers and we unhesitatingly pronounce him to be the best we have heard, not even excepting the late Daniel O'Connell'.

This was a considerable compliment from Sheahan whose Irish patriotism was clearly evident in his account of the 1836 visit of 'that highly gifted and much abused member of the English legislature, Daniel O'Connell'. He quoted both from O'Connell's reply to the invitation from Hull in which he referred to 'the six centuries of misrule with which his country had been affected' and, with obvious approval, from his speech at the Public Rooms which 'was full of patriotic sentiment and a splendid display of oratory'.

Sheahan's history of Hull was printed and published by John Green of Beverley, and proved so popular that a second edition was issued in 1866. His other works included a *Guide to Beverley*, *An Antiquarian Ramble Through Beverley*, first published in the *Beverley Guardian*, and according to the title page of his history of Hull, 'Histories of Cambridgeshire, Oxfordshire, the East and North Ridings of Yorkshire, Boroughbridge, etc.'

From Tiger Lane, he moved to Newbegin, also in Beverley, where much of his historical work was done, but later he returned to Hull, where he died at his home, 55 Blake Street, in 1893. The information he gave on St. Charles suggested a link with that church, though his funeral service was conducted by Father Ryan in the Catholic part of the Western Cemetery, and by the 'express wish of himself and his friends the funeral was in every way an unpretending one'. As a great historian of Hull, it is fitting that a brass plaque to his memory was erected in Holy Trinity Church.

Mark Sykes, 1879-1919

Mark Sykes has the distinction of being the first Catholic M.P. for Hull since the Reformation. Yet, in spite of this unique record, he was following a long family tradition of service to the port from which much of its wealth derived. The Sykes had the foresight to anticipate the great commercial potential which Hull was to offer ambitious merchants as the economy of northern England expanded under the impulse of the Industrial Revolution. Hull was ideally placed for the import of raw materials from northern Europe and the export of finished goods as well as a flourishing coastal trade.

In the late 17th century, William Sykes moved from Leeds to Hull, where the family prospered, rising so confidently through the échelons of civic office that within a century his descendants had become powerful figures in Georgian Hull. William's grandson, Richard, married Mary, the daughter of another merchant, Mark Kirby, whose land at Sledmere was to become the Sykes' stronghold in the Wolds, while the son of Richard's second marriage, Joseph, who moved to Westella and became the head of the cadet branch of the Sykes, acquired great wealth through his virtual monopoly of the import of Swedish iron ore and massive influence through his membership of Hull Corporation.

His sons followed his example of public service, particularly his sixth son, Daniel, a highly-principled Whig M.P. for Hull, 1820-30, who was a committed reformer opposing slavery and naval impressment, and a courageous advocate of religious toleration. Though one forebear had been canonised as St. Edmund Sykes in the 16th century, Daniel followed what had become the Anglican tradition of both senior and junior branches of

the family, but, while his personal preference was for extremely Low Church worship, he defended himself in memorable words when he was attacked in staunchly Protestant Hull for his support for Catholic Emancipation: 'I do not see why I should deny to others the toleration I claim for myself.' Ironically, in view of the popularity of the Catholic Mark Sykes in the 20th century, it was Daniel Sykes' pro-Catholic sympathy which proved too advanced for his Protestant electors and resulted in

Sir Mark Sykes

his decision not to defend his vulnerable seat in 1830 but to move to another constituency, Beverley.

Mark Sykes was a member of the senior branch of the family, the Sykes of Sledmere, which had acquired a baronetcy in 1783. His father was Sir Tatton, the fifth baronet, but, it was his mother to whom he owed the Catholic Faith which was to be passed on to and be maintained by his descendants. Born Jessica Cavendish-Bentinck, she was beautiful, wild and irrepressible but with an instinct for charity and religion which her behaviour concealed but never submerged. In 1882 she was received into the Catholic Church at Brompton Oratory and three-year-old Mark, who had been baptised 'a ministello heretico' in the old parish church at Sledmere, 'was unwittingly received into the Faith which he so valiantly defended in years to come against the hosts of heretics and scoffers'. His father remained an Anglican, though he had strong Catholic sympathies. Temperamental differences between the reclusive, inhibited Tatton and the flighty, extrovert Jessica did not make for a happy marriage, and the conflict between two warring parents resulted in a rocky course of education for a highly intelligent boy who read widely and deeply but not systematically. 'I never had a childhood,' he later explained, and school terms at Beaumont were interrupted by long visits abroad with one or other parent. This was an obvious handicap in preparing for examinations but it did provide an exceptional knowledge and understanding of foreign countries, particularly of the Near East, which were to prove a considerable asset when he entered the Commons.

Mark left Cambridge without taking a degree, but in the years before he became an M.P. he was far from idle. He served with the East Yorkshire militia in South Africa during the Boer War, he wrote three books on his travels, acted as private secretary to George Wyndham, the Irish Secretary, and served as an honorary attaché to the British Embassy in Turkey.

A number of Sykes had already been M.P.s for Yorkshire constituencies. In addition to Daniel (Hull 1820-30, Beverley 1830-31), there was Christopher (Beverley 1784-90) Mark Masterman (York 1807-20), and Mark's uncle, Christopher (Beverley 1865-8, East Riding 1868-1885 and Buckrose 1885-92). Yet in spite of this roll of honour to act as a spur, Mark was not enthusiastic about entering politics. 'People want me to go into Parliament at the next general election, which I consider in every way ridiculous,' he wrote in 1900, giving as his reasons his ignorance and his reluctance to become mere lobby fodder in the growing party voting machines. 'The more I read of Parliament, the more firmly convinced am I that I am not intended for such a career,' he repeated the following year when he had been approached by some individuals to stand as a

Conservative in Buckrose, the natural constituency for a Sykes as it included Sledmere. 'I have told them that I am neither *a buffoon, an office seeker, nor a hypocrite*, that I cannot talk sonorous twaddle for endless hours, that I have neither a large stomach nor a white waistcoat, and am in fact in no way fitted for a local magnate . . .'

His political career was to show that his personal preference was for the more romantic version of Tory democracy in which the members of a close-knit society were bound to each other by a common moral code of mutual responsibilities and duties. 'I stand for industrial peace and friendship between Capital and Labour,' he pronounced on a later occasion. His background, his financial independence and his status enabled him to rise above the fray and to view issues in their widest perspective, always from the stance of a statesman uninvolved in the detailed discussion of domestic issues which were the natural concern of less visionary backbenchers. Yet his privileged position did not make him insensitive to the acute problems suffered by the less fortunate or the urgent need for massive social reform. The sight of unemployed men walking from Hull and Liverpool to Sledmere in search of work proved to him the need for Labour Exchanges some years before they were established, he was highly critical of bad landlords and he studied at first-hand the working conditions of fishermen and the squalid environment of children brought up in the slums of Hull. He was not blind to the attractions of the Labour Party for working men and said that if he had been poor he would have been a supporter. But it was as a Conservative that he stood in the two general elections of 1910 in his home constituency of Buckrose. A reporter who interviewed him at Sledmere shortly before the meeting at Nafferton at which he declared his intention to stand, described him in words which vividly convey both his appearance and his personality: 'Slim, tall, alert, wire and whipcord and nerves, a clear Anglo-Saxon countenance and a fair moustache, this is Mark Sykes, heir to the vast Sledmere estate, and still on the very sunny side of 30. What he does he does thoroughly and, when I found him, he was putting the finishing touches to the lecture he was to deliver at Driffield on the morrow.'

The lustre attached to the name of Sykes and the deferential voting habits of that period could not, however, overcome the strong preference of the many Nonconformists in the constituency for the Liberal candidate, Luke White, a Driffield solicitor, and on both occasions Sykes was defeated by small majorities. He was, though, far from depressed and dismissed his failures with patrician disdain: 'If you choose to give me a political career I will take it up, but, if not, I have my books and I can go back to my plough.' George Wyndham advised him to stick with Buckrose unless 'an absolutely gilt-edged security in an important constituency' should materialise elsewhere. The possibility of a seat at Horncastle was mooted, but electors there were as Nonconformist as those in Buckrose and the idea was taken no further.

Yet, events were moving Sykes' way. In 1910 Sir Henry Seymour King, Tory M.P. for Central Hull since 1885, had been re-elected by 3,624 votes against his Liberal opponent's 3,418. But that was not the end of the matter. The Liberals claimed that King had been plying his supporters and their families with too many treats and that his victory had been gained by unlawful means. A petition claiming that the election was invalid was successful, King was debarred from ever again standing in the constituency and a by-election was, therefore, called to find his replacement. The verdict on King dismissed any allegations that he had acted corruptly and there was considerable feeling in the constituency that the judgement was unfair and that Central Hull had been wrongly deprived of a very popular Member. As a Tory-held seat for 25 years there was great determination among local activists not only to retain it in a by-election but to adopt an exceptionally strong candidate who could dispel any unpleasant aftermath of the affair and vindicate Sir Henry's honour.

Mark Sykes was the ideal man. The name of Sykes always rang with éclat in Hull, and Mark was already known there when he was still a boy, accompanying his mother when she provided her annual treat to Hull's Catholic schools, and being popular with the children. On occasions he had attended St. Charles church.

The Conservative press hailed him as 'a Paladin of his Party – as a young Knight errant of uncommon gifts and of high and honourable renown'. It was an image which events would never tarnish. For the moment he was adopted (officially as a Unionist), he was a new star in the political firmament and a euphoric article honoured his achievements: 'By his close associations with Hull and the East Riding, by his versatility, his personality, his interest in social reform, his sympathy with the poorer classes, he has endeared himself on all hands. Already his name is a household word in Hull.'

As a wealthy landowner Mark Sykes had to defend himself from the attacks of opponents who claimed that he was abusing his unfair economic clout. He did so with good humour and sincerity: 'It might seem impossible and incredible to the Liberals that he was not a natural oppressor of the people, with his hands and arms stained in gore up to the elbow in grinding the people down, always seeking to inflate his own pocket. He knew that those who knew him and his family believed that what he said he really meant.' Always aiming to get to the truth and heart of an issue, he gave his perceptive and stirring conclusion: 'It was his absolute conviction that they must improve the condition of the people of this country if the Empire was to remain great and realise its destiny.'

At another meeting, he asked rhetorically and provocatively, 'Supposing that Bismarck came to Hull and supposing that Hull was a Prussian town of thirty years ago, would he not be shocked?' Bismarck was a social reformer, and Sykes continued: 'Would he not be tempted at seeing the condition in which a large mass of people were in this town today?' It was terrible to him 'to see the destitution, the misery, the depravity in the back streets of Hull', in his view a situation produced by free trade.

It was a by-election which had every reason to arouse immense interest and it was fought in unusual conditions, against the background of a bitterly fought dock strike and with an interlude for the coronation of George V. On completion of polling Mark Sykes was declared the winner, with 3,823 votes to his Liberal opponent's 3,545, a majority of 278. Though in a letter to his wife he described his entry into the Chamber of the Commons as 'very funny', he was clearly happy with his reception. The first person to congratulate him was his old adversary, Luke White, and 'The Speaker seemed really pleased'.

His maiden speech (27 November 1911), on foreign affairs, with particular reference to the Near East, was listened to in a rare silence and then loudly cheered, and he was immediately congratulated by the Prime Minister, Asquith, a triumph which he modestly denigrated as no more than a series of lucky accidents. The previous speaker had been so boring that the House was ready to cheer anything, he knew his subject, it was not controversial, and it so happened that the Prime Minster – another Yorkshireman – was the next to speak. Of all the Tories who lived in the Buckrose Division, it was said, he was the only one who had not lost his head over the maiden speech!

'There was something piquant in a Yorkshire member specialising in the East', wrote his biographer, Shane Leslie. But this was not a period when M.P.s received large postbags each day full of letters from constituents seeking authoritative help with their problems. Nor was it expected that a M.P. would be seen regularly in his constituency. There were no 'surgeries', and visits on special occasions sufficed. Sykes' hosting of a reception at the Assembly Rooms in 1912 was an event which enabled him to thank electors and to keep his seat warm for the next round. The welcome he and his wife received showed how well he had sustained his popularity: his activities on a wider stage, both nationally and internationally, reflected vicarious honour on his supporters and on Hull itself. Most of his routine constituency matters were handled by the Conservative agent, Councillor

W. H. Cooper (son of the more famous Sir Henry Cooper), and, in view of Sir Henry Seymour King's bitter experience, careful accounts were kept of the donations to good causes which M.P.s were expected to support. He had a particular interest in the Catholic Boys' Home and became a member of the Hull Circle of the Catenian Society.

On his arrival at Westminster he was immediately recognised as a member of unusual quality and potential who 'had no difficulty in gaining from the first the ear of the House of Commons'. He was inexperienced in parliamentary ways, but he was no nervous newcomer anxious to gain the Whips' approval, and his unusual approach to political matters had a freshness which proved an invigorating contrast to the tired routine of party political point-scoring. Strongly traditionalist in his support for the House of Lords and the merits of the private ownership of land, he was uninhibited by party dogma or by the vested interests of one sector of society and earned himself the soubriquet 'M.P. for England'. So impressed was one Hull Radical that he felt impelled to write to the *[Hull] Daily Mail:* 'Oh, Sir Mark, you have a great place in the great heart of England. We are all brothers, no matter what our clan.'

Sykes was no tub-thumper or master of histrionic gestures. He spoke quietly, almost as if he were thinking aloud, an untidy lock of hair falling over his forehead and eyes gleaming. Any suggestion of casualness, though, would have been misleading. He was not an impromptu participator in debates but prepared carefully for the occasions when he intended to speak and delivered his words with authority, almost ignoring any relationship they had with the rest of the debate.

A brilliant vignette of Mark Sykes, the orator, written anonymously by 'A Back Bencher' and reproduced locally at the time of his death, captured his individualistic style: 'He tumbles out his words. His brain works like a mill-race and his tongue can hardly keep pace with it. His is a case of thought leaping out to wed with thought ere thought could wed itself with speech. His attitude is peculiar. He leans, half doubled up, over the bench in front of him, his head thrust forward, his arms extended in rapid gestures, now in expostulation, now persuasive. There is nothing in the House that is quite like it.' His range, however, enabled him to move from the heights of rhetoric to the 'light and farcical' as occasion demanded; his wit tended to be in that rather cavalier vein popular with gentlemanly audiences in the Edwardian period.

Religion was an integral part of his life and he was as instinctively Catholic as if he had been descended from an old family of devout Recusants. He prayed intensely and lengthily and believed that prayers were – eventually – answered, attended Mass daily and had the Blessed

Sacrament reserved in Sledmere House. Yet his unusual background, his travels and his sheer intelligence gave him a profound respect for other Christian churches and for other faiths. All religions, he believed, contained some truth, and, in an increasingly secular world, a limited truth was preferable to its complete absence. He was attracted by the philosophy and spirituality of eastern religions: Moslems, he considered, often shamed Christians by their concern for the poor and by the strength of their devotions. His own faith was so strong that he could at times treat religious matters with a lightness and a humour which are often the signs of the truly devout.

He made no attempt to conceal his Catholicism and he was aware that it aroused both interest and curiosity. But, while totally committed to his Faith, he never discussed aspects of his inner life in which others had no right to intervene. For his time he was a man of remarkably advanced attitudes, particularly on the Irish question, as highly controversial then as it remains today, with Unionists and Nationalists opposed but in a still united Ireland. His aim was always to encourage understanding between the two sides, and his rare, if not unique, position as a Catholic Unionist M.P. who could appreciate the strength of Irish Nationalist aspirations ensured that he spoke with total fairness and with mature wisdom. 'It is not a question of right or wrong,' he said. 'It's a question of two ships in a fog trying to avoid a collision.' He considered it as despicable to insult the green flag as the Union Jack, and in words which a modern politician would echo he described the only possible way to a solution: 'The essential to a settlement is that there shall be no victory.'

In what has been described as his most memorable speech, on 31 March 1914, he dismissed the tired arguments of those who showed that they had learnt nothing from history: 'I feel that the blame must be upon us all. We have drifted on passions, and both sides have gone from one wild cry to another until we have divided class from class, creed from creed, in order to further our policies, until at the very end of it all one cannot deny that the military forces and the very Throne itself have been involved in our quarrels.'

As a member of the party which defended the Union at a time when his more gun-happy colleagues were ready to use force in defence of their opinions, Sykes took a courageously independent line when he defended Irish Catholics against charges of intolerance: 'Those who call upon the people of England and Ulster to fight against Home Rule, because Catholics will abuse the liberties of Protestants, are doing an ill-service to the cause of Christianity and the cause of Unionism. To transform the bulwarks of belief into battering rams of mutual destruction seems to deny every rule of policy, sense or propriety.'

He also defended the Irish clergy from charges of wielding despotic power. On the contrary, he wrote, in a moving tribute, they had been the brave supporters of the poor in the most difficult of times: 'The native Irish found in the Catholic priesthood a friend, who alone remained to console the dying, to bury the dead, to help the living to live, and this in spite of proscription, penal laws and a whole library of inhuman statutes and enactments . . . In the foulest slums the Irish priest goes fearless of sickness and contagion. In the heat of England's battle it is an Irish priest who gives courage to English Catholic soldiers.'

He became an authority on Zionism, his initial opposition turning to support in the latter part of his life. It was in Hull that he publicly announced his conclusion that a settled Jewish national home 'would mean that every Jew throughout the world would be made more valuable to the state which he had chosen for himself'. His biographer, Shane Leslie, has commented: 'It was his Catholicism which assisted Mark to understand the Jewish tragedy. He was interested in the ethos of the real Hebrew, not in the Anglicized Jew.' In London in 1917 he spoke in visionary terms of his hopes: 'It might be the destiny of the Jewish race to be the bridge between Asia and Europe, to bring the spirituality of Asia to Europe and the vitality of Europe to Asia.'

Though early death robbed Sykes of what gave every indication of a distinguished career as a statesman, by an irony of history his name has received international recognition for what, against his wishes, is known as the Sykes-Picot Treaty (1916) between Britain, France and Russia concerning Syria, Mesopotamia and Eastern Asia Minor, 'a secret pact providing for the partition of the Ottoman Empire after the war'.

Sykes was acutely aware of the country's vulnerability in the event of war and the consequent need to be well prepared in time of peace by developing a trained territorial army. Putting his beliefs into practice in 1913, he began raising the famous Wagoners' Reserve, formed of farm workers on the Wolds, experienced in handling horses pulling pole-wagons, who would, he considered, be invaluable as drivers in a future war. The foreign menace which he had long foreseen became a reality on 4 August 1914 and, as part of the BEF, Sykes' Wagoners were the first civilians to serve overseas.

Mark Sykes was abroad when the general election was fought in 1918, and it was from Jerusalem that he sent his election address to the electors of Central Hull, 'surely the first ever sent to an English constituency from the Holy City'. He had succeeded to the baronetcy on the death of his father in 1913, and his wife, Lady Sykes, née Edith Gorst, was the one who managed his campaign in Hull. He was in Aleppo when the news of his success reached him and in return he sent her a cable of touching gratitude:

'Adjutrix mea et liberatrix mea es tu' [You are my helper and my deliverer]. In his message to his electors he expressed his hope to be in Hull at the first opportunity.

It was not to be. In Paris for the Versailles Peace Conference, he died, after a short illness on 16 February 1919, a victim of the influenza pandemic,

On 22 February a Requiem Mass was held at St. Charles church. The shock of such an unexpected death had a particular poignancy for Hull Catholics, who had so recently found such an outstanding spokesman. They were reluctant to sever the link which promised so much and Lady Sykes was invited to stand for the vacant seat, but she refused on the grounds of her duty to her six young children. If she had accepted, she could well have made history as the first woman to sit in the House of Commons. Catholics throughout the country realised that they had lost a leading layman and *The Universe* described Sykes' death as the most prominent loss to English Catholics since the death of the Duke of Norfolk.

He was brought back to Sledmere for burial. The village has two war memorials, one for the Wagoners, which he had designed on his last visit to Sledmere, and the Eleanor Cross, set up by his father, which was made into a memorial to other victims of the war. One panel remained empty, and the figure of a Crusader with the words, *'Laetare Jerusalem'* [Jerusalem, rejoice] was now added in memory of Mark Sykes himself.

Bibliography
S. Leslie, *Mark Sykes: His Life and Letters* (1923).
R. Adelson, *Mark Sykes – Portrait of an Amateur* (1975).
C. S. Sykes, *The Visitor's Book* (1978).
Dictionary of National Biography.
(Hull) *Daily Mail.*

The Farrell Family

The story of the Farrell Family in East Yorkshire is one of remarkable upward mobility in a relatively short time, progress which is further support for the thesis that, in spite of admitted disadvantages and overt prejudice in the 19th and early 20th centuries, Catholics of ability and determination were able to enjoy success in professional careers and become influential members of the local establishment.

The first member of the family to arrive in the area was James, who left Ireland about 1835, and, after a period as a dyer in the West Riding, and later as a hawker and travelling bookseller, moved to Hull and began business in Savile Street as a bookseller and stationer.

Thomas Frederick Farrell, 1849-1930. Solicitor and Registrar of Hull County Court.
(By kind permission of T. H. F. Farrell, Esq.)

In 1849 Thomas Frederick Farrell was born in Hull, the fourth son of James and his wife, Elizabeth, and it was Thomas's talent, fortuitously detected at an early age, which led to the Farrell's elevation from trade to the legal profession in which they were to earn a high reputation. Thomas owed the foundation of his success to St. Charles School, Pryme Street, where he inspired sufficient faith in his potential to ensure that he continued his education at Ushaw College, which catered for lay students as well as seminarians, and, as it was affiliated to London University, provided the opportunity to gain an external London B.A. degree. Thomas did well at Ushaw, for which he always retained great affection, matriculating in 1867 and graduating in 1868.

After Ushaw, he started writing for the *Hull Morning News* but also began his articles with Rollit & Sons, solicitors, in 1875, working both at their London and Hull offices. He was admitted a solicitor in 1878, the year in which the firm moved to Cogan House, Bowlalley Lane. He was, apparently to those not familiar with him, a rather austere, even terrifying, figure, but beneath this daunting facade was a kind and friendly personality. Although regarded as a confirmed bachelor, when he was 30 he married Monica Mary Collingwood, a member of another Hull Catholic family, and their marriage of over 50 years produced five sons and a daughter.

The eldest son, Bede, born in 1881, went, like father, to Ushaw, but for health reasons was brought home and sent in 1894 to the newly opened Hymers College. In 1900 he started his articles with Rollit & Sons, was admitted in 1905, and, in 1910 became a partner in what was now Rollit & Co. Internal problems in the firm, however, resulted in Bede Farrell setting up his own independent practice in 1913. He was a keen member of the Territorials and, although he refused a commission in the regular army, volunteered for overseas duty on the outbreak of war in 1914. Just over six months later he was killed in the Battle of Ypres.

His brother, Hugh, born in 1888, the fourth of the Farrell sons, was educated at Hymers College where, in addition to taking a full part in extra-curriculuar activities, he won an open Classical scholarship to Jesus College, Cambridge, and was a Hymers exhibitioner, graduating with honours in the Classical and Law Tripos. In 1913 he was admitted a solicitor and in 1915 became a partner in the firm which afterwards was re-named Rollit & Farrell. Two years later he married Maria van den Bergh, a Belgian refugee who had escaped from the Siege of Antwerp. The death of his father, Thomas, in 1930 and the acceptance of a new partner, John Dickinson Bladon, led to a further enlargement of the firm's name to Rollit Farrell & Bladon.

Hugh, another outwardly forbidding figure, but highly regarded by his colleagues and for 17 years Honorary Secretary of the Incorporated Law Society, died in 1959 aged 70, and it was his son, Thomas Hugh Francis, born in 1930, who was to continue the family's legal tradition. After school at Ampleforth, Tom, as he is generally known, entered into his articles in 1947 and, in view of his father's ill health and the need to do his national service, enrolled at the same time for a law degree at the University College of Hull. He graduated in 1950, was admitted a solicitor, and became a partner in 1952, before joining the army.

After his return to civilian life he retained his military links by serving with the Territorials, as well as taking a leading part in local public life, standing as a Conservative parliamentary candidate in West Hull and becoming one of Hull's youngest sheriffs in 1960. His religious allegiance was demonstrated in his voluntary work as Governor of both Endsleigh College of Education and the Marist College, founder member of Hull University Catholic Chaplaincy Association, and Chairman of the Frank Finn Homes of Rest. His distinguished public career has included his appointment as Deputy Lieutenant for the East Riding, Pro-Chancellor of Hull University, the conferment of an honorary doctorate by the University, and the award of the C.B.E.

In 1964 Tom Farrell married the Hon. Clodagh Morris, younger daughter of Lord Morris, and great-granddaughter of a man who had emigrated to Canada at the time of the Famine in the 1840s. The story had been brought full circle.

The Farrells have now been associated with Hull and East Yorkshire for 150 years and their history provides an illuminating commentary on the development of English society – not least the status of Catholics within, and their contribution to, that society during the past century and a half.

Bibliography

I acknowledge with gratitude the valuable information contained in Dr. T. H. F. Farrell's book, *A Brief History: Rollit Farrell & Bladon, Solicitors, 1841-1991* (Hull 1991).
Other sources used are the *East Riding Bystander* (Vol. 1 No. 3, March 1970) and the *Hull Times*.

Joseph Henry Hirst, 1863-1945

Joseph Henry Hirst is a man whose local fame falls far short of his achievements. As the highly talented first City Architect 1900-26, he has had a lasting impact on the appearance of Hull, and the quality of his work is recognised by architectural experts.

Born at South Milford in 1863 in what had originally been a gentry

family but which had
suffered financially
through its adherence to
its Catholic faith, he was
the only son of William
Hirst, who worked for 13
years for the North
Eastern Railway before
being 'covenanted out' to India, where, in addition to his normal long-distance journeys, he had the honour of driving 'nearly all the vice-regal specials that have come my way', including the Prince and Princess of Wales (later Edward VII and Queen Alexandra) on their last run before embarking for England. His forebears had similar records of railway service: William's maternal grandfather had worked on the construction of the Hull-Selby line, and his father, another North Eastern employee, had died 'in harness' at the age of 72.

In his final years William lived in Hull, and an obituary in the *Catholic Magazine* of February 1918, subtitled 'St. Vincent's Notes', paid a moving tribute to 'two valuable and zealous members of the congregation' who had died in the previous month, Edward Dixon and William himself: 'Mr. Hirst was one of those old Catholics, very few of whom we have with us today, who was always most faithful to the Church, never late for service, and up to a few months of his death a most regular attender. Even in his spare time, as a very capable amateur carver of wood, his piety and devotion showed itself in the crucifixes and objects of devotion he so delighted to make.'

Instead of following the family tradition of railway service, his son, Joseph Henry Hirst, chose a career in architecture. Information about his early education is not so far available, but, probably at the age of 14, he was articled to W. H. Wellsted, and was clearly a pupil who had found the perfect niche. In 1880, when he was only 17, he had his first drawing and design, for a country residence, published in a newspaper, *The House Decorator*; in 1883, when he was 20, *The Illustrated Carpenter and Builder* published his drawing of a town residence; and in 1884 he submitted a drawing and design for industrial dwellings which was published in the same journal and which earned him a prize and a medal. He travelled widely to pursue his passion for architecture and at the age of 21 took up employment with Hull Corporation.

From 1886-93 he served as a volunteer engineer in the Humber Volunteer Division of Submarine Mariners of the Royal Engineers, and a photograph shows a dapper young man of 23 proudly wearing his sergeant major's uniform. His former employer, Major (later Colonel) Wellsted, was the commander of the division, and it is likely that Wellsted's example was the inspiration for Hirst's decision to enrol.

It was an opportune time to be an architect in Hull. The town and port were expanding rapidly, Victorian and Edwardian civic leaders, businessmen and industrialists were proud of what they had achieved, and their aim was to commission buildings which would symbolise their confidence, their optimism and their success. The granting of city status in 1897 was another boost to their esteem, and when the new City of Hull decided to appoint its first City Architect, their employee, Hirst, who must already have proved his worth, was the ideal candidate with the imagination and ability to provide buildings of appropriate dignity. His appointment also made him the first city architect in the country.

The most famous of all his buildings is the City Hall, designed in the Italianate Baroque style, with a dome which forms a familiar part of Hull's impressive skyline, and with an interior which adds to the dignity of important ceremonies and events. Yet, while it was under construction, it was 'the subject of a lot of debate and not a little criticism'. Hirst cheerfully rode the storm, 'outwardly unperturbed by the comments of those who knew nothing about buildings'. The finished product silenced his critics, and ever after it remained 'the joy and pride of its designer'.

So lengthy is the list of his buildings that one can only be amazed at his sustained level of achievement and his versatility. The roll of honour includes the former Central Police Station, the Market Hall, Beverley Road

J. H. Hirst's design for the City Hall, Hull
(Audrey Howes)

Baths (and probably Holderness Road Baths), and the Tuberculosis Sanatorium, Cottingham (the embryo of the later Castle Hill complex), as well as some which have earned particular praise from experts, the 'delightful' Carnegie Library and the 'charming' Pickering Almshouses, along with the old Museum of Fisheries.

It was also a time of significant educational progress, and Joseph Hirst took a major part in creating fine new buildings for students and pupils. Endsleigh College, the Nautical School in the Boulevard, Sidmouth Street, Southcoates and Villa Place Schools are all examples of the quality and range of his work. Another one, Newland High School (1914), was so admired by one woman on the staff that she always described it as 'the last good building erected in Hull'.

From his early days as City Architect, Hirst was involved in council schemes for housing Hull's growing working class population, many of whom lived in grossly sub-standard dwellings. In 1900 Hull's first flats were erected in Great Passage Street, and Hirst was responsible for the first working-class houses in the City, in Newbridge Road, and for three housing estates, Cottingham Road, Hessle Road (near Pickering Park) and Preston Road.

Inevitably there were other, more mundane, projects, among them the Fish Market on Corporation Field, the Disinfectant Station in Scarborough Street, together with stables and cart sheds for the Sanitary Department, lodges for East and West Parks and greenhouses, and a number of cabmen's shelters. None was spectacular but all were undertaken with his characteristic attention to detail and observance of the highest standards. A photograph of the Empress Public House had a caption in his own neat writing: 'This building, originally a warehouse, was cut through to make Alfred Gelder Street. This new front was built and the building converted into the Empress Inn'. Outside Hull, Hirst worked on two Catholic buildings, Crossbeck Convent, Normanby, and the Convent of Mercy at Ormesby.

Although an architect with his own ideas who did not feel the need to slavishly copy the buildings of the past, Hirst had a proper respect for the inheritance of architectural achievement handed on from previous generations, and he could be scathing in his criticism of what he considered inappropriate designs. One which roused his fury and revealed the intensity of his faith was a proposed Catholic church at Beckenham, Kent, designed by H. Spence Sales and A. N. Tucker to be constructed in re-inforced concrete. So incensed was Hirst that he wrote to his distant relation, Cardinal Hinsley, the Archbishop of Westminster, on 8 October 1935:

'We Catholics are proud of our traditions, but, alas, some architects now design our churches merely to be novel, to catch the eye, to become notorious – it is the spirit of the age– a craving for novelty and advertisement.

'Contrast these monstrosities with the churches which our forefathers built, the cathedrals and parish churches which we see in all our great towns and even in the most remote villages.

'Although these buildings have not been used for Catholic worship for 400 years, as soon as you enter you feel an atmosphere of reverence and devotion which is altogether absent in any of these ultramodern churches.

'Will such an atmosphere be found in this proposed structure at Beckenham: I cannot call it a church, nor the House of God. A Catholic church should impress non Catholics with its dignity, just as our unchanging ritual does. But churches designed like that at Beckenham will only provoke derision and laughter. Strangers would never think of looking for the true church in structures such as this.

'With all the progress which is supposed to have been made in art and design, and with all the great examples of church architecture left to us, architects ought surely to be able to improve upon the work of their predecessors. But do they? Ninety per cent of so called design in architecture, sculpture and painting is pure rubbish. The modern movement in architecture is nothing more than a disease, common sense and development have gone to the wall.

'In my humble opinion, one reason for these ugly structures is because modern architects have lost the art of design, they are incapable of making an original drawing and can only produce a succession of straight lines which, when carried out, give a bald flatness, enormous chilly windows, horizontal bars and flat roofs. Are such buildings the best we can erect to the honour and glory of Almighty God? Surely it is an insult to the Real Presence to be housed in a permanent building as stark and bare as the proposed church at Beckenham. To me it would seem to be a sacrilege to celebrate Mass in a warehouse like that, and a shocking waste of £12,000 which is to be the cost of the building.

'I have a very strong opinion that a church should look like a church, just as a cinema should look like a cinema, but no one looking at the Beckenham building would guess what it was; and this reminds me of an experience of my own. I was looking at a

Catholic church during construction when a gentlemen, a total stranger, stopped and asked me if I liked the style and said that, passing it every day, he had taken it for a cinema until he was told that it was to be a Catholic church. From that I gathered that he had a very poor opinion of Catholics, simply because of that building.

'There is no doubt that churches should be designed with the old Catholic feeling, and our traditions religiously maintained, or improved upon if possible. Why cannot architects give us something to be proud of, and why should a parish be inflicted with a permanent eyesore?

'From my 50 years of practical experience I know that something more dignified, more impressive and more Catholic could be built for £12,000.

'To ensure that the Catholic Church in England shall have only of the best, would it not be possible for the Archbishop to appoint a small committee of priests with experience in church design, to whom all plans for all churches should be submitted for consideration and approval before building contracts are entered into?

'I am writing very strongly, for which I must ask Your Grace's forgiveness. It is not that I want to dictate or even interfere. I am prompted only by a sincere desire to see new churches equal in design to those erected in the ages of Faith, churches which even today are the admiration of all, Catholic and non-Catholic alike. There is no reason why new Catholic churches should not be admired today. It is only a question of design, not of expense.'

Cardinal Hinsley replied the day he received the letter expressing his 'full agreement' and referring to Pius XI's criticism of 'such enormities'. It was possible, said the Cardinal, for churches to be 'majestic in their simplicity', and he went further: 'Personally I find it quite out of proportion to build costly churches when the living stone, immortal souls, are perishing for want of opportunities to learn the faith!' Hirst also replied by return of post: 'If I have been able to do anything to assist in stopping the rot in Catholic Church design, then I feel that I have not lived my life in vain.'

Joseph Hirst's ancestors had all married into other Catholic families, and the marriage of a great-aunt, Sarah Saul, to Thomas Hinsley had created the valued link with Cardinal Arthur Hinsley. He took a keen interest in family history, and his scrapbook includes notes on the origin of his

surname, references to people of the same name which he had gleaned from his perusal of old documents, particularly those who had fallen foul of penal legislation. Hirst's papers reveal his continuing interest in, and high regard for, Saint Thomas More. His private office in Percy Street was named More's Chambers and he gave a stained glass window depicting the saint to St. Charles church.

In 1895 his paper, 'The Castle of Kingston upon Hull', was published in the Transactions of the East Riding Antiquarian Society, and this led to his most important academic work, a book, *The Blockhouses of Kingston upon Hull and Who Lived There*,

Canon Francis J. Hall of St. Charles Borromeo. (Diocese of Middlesbrough)

subtitled, *A Glimpse of Catholic Life in the Penal Times – a Missing Page of Local History*, published in 1913 for the author by A. Brown and Sons, with an epigraph on its title page from his hero, Thomas More ('You have yet the faith still, and intend to keep it alway'), and an introduction by Canon Francis J. Hall of St. Charles church. Profits from the sale of the book were to be devoted to the support of St. Vincent's Orphan Boys' Home. He had a life-long association both with St. Charles church and with Canon (later Monsignor) Francis J. Hall.

To Hirst it was a tragic irony that the defences which were built on the east side of the River, in obedience to Henry VIII's command that Hull should be made 'mighty strong', incorporated stone from St. Mary's, Lowgate (which had suffered damage), and from Hull's Blackfriary, Whitefriary and Carthusian Priory as well as from the Cistercian Priory of Swine: 'Little did these friars think when erecting their religious houses in Hull that the very stones, wherewith their friaries had been constructed, nay, even their own grave covers, would one day form part of the walls of the dungeons in which were to be imprisoned and tortured innocent men and women professing the Faith which the friars themselves had done so much to preserve.'

Although written from a consciously partisan stance, and with a fervency of tone which seems dated in a more ecumenical climate, Hirst's work retains great value as a careful and detailed study containing the results of his extensive researches to uncover such information as is available about the fates of those who suffered for their religion and who deserve to be honoured as individuals, not lost in the impersonality of statistics.

Hull's Tudor defences consisted of a north and south blockhouse and a central castle, and Hirst paints a vividly horrifying picture of the conditions in these military buildings used for accommodating Catholic prisoners who refused to abandon their beliefs and practices. There were no executions in Hull, but a number were taken from Hull to be put to death, among them two of the earliest prisoners, John Rochester and James Wannant, monks from the Charterhouse in London (1536), and two priests, Edmund Sykes (1587) and John Hewitt (1588), all executed in York.

Among the numbers confined in these appalling circumstances Hirst included: Dr. Thomas Vavasour, a member of an old Yorkshire family, 'a doctor of physic, a great scholar, and a man of much eloquence of speech'; Mrs. Anne Lander, a descendant of the Constable's; Thomas Madde (or Mudd) and John Almond, both monks from Jervaulx; Mrs. Anne Teshe, arrested at the same time as Margaret Clitherow; Thomas Clitherow, brother-in-law of the York martyr; and John Towneley of Towneley Hall, Lancashire, a member of a landed family which, after Emancipation, gave Beverley a Catholic M.P., another John Towneley, 1841-52.

'Uncle Joe', as he was known to his colleagues, resigned in 1926 after 42 years service with Hull Corporation. He was in good health, but, with commendable magnanimity, believed that, as there was a tremendous amount of work ahead, Hull would be wise to appoint a younger man. He did, however, continue privately as a consultant architect and there is a family tradition that he was offered a partnership by another Hull architect, Alfred Gelder.

After living in Derringham Street he moved to York Cottage, Hymers Avenue, and later to 47 Hymers Avenue. When this final Hull home was bombed in the last war, he moved to Selby, and it was there he died in May 1945. He has no statue, but words on the memorial to Sir Christopher Wren in London could apply equally to Joseph Hirst in Hull: 'If you are seeking my memorial look around you.'

Bibliography

In preparing this biographical study I was greatly assisted by Joseph Henry Hirst's granddaughter, Mrs. Audrey Howes, who generously lent me her grandfather's books and papers and provided some useful oral information. His obituary appeared in the *Hull and Yorkshire Times*, 19 May 1945. In addition to the two publications mentioned in the above section, J. H. Hirst also wrote *The Armorial Bearings of Kingston upon Hull* (Hull 1916).

Memories of a Catholic Girlhood

by
John Markham

This is a book which has tried to survey Hull's Catholic history with the objectivity which every academic study requires, and the number of subjects covered and the detail which have to be contained in a limited space inevitably result in the need to summarise and make generalisations. But each person's life is unique, and focusing on one local Catholic, born before the First World War, is, I hope, an acceptable way of capturing something of the flavour of religious life in Hull in the early part of the century now coming to an end. It is based on interviews I have had with Dorothy Stutt, who has written for local newspapers for nearly 60 years, and, in her 92nd year still contributes to the Beverley Advertiser, *a record which in 1998 earned her the M.B.E.*

Although Dorothy spent almost all her early life in Hull, she was born in South Bank, Middlesbrough, in 1907 and was evacuated there to stay with her devoutly Catholic relatives during the First World War, a decision which she now considers curious in view of the industry and shipyards which might have attracted enemy raiders.

Dorothy was the offspring of what used to be called 'a mixed marriage' and her Catholic faith came through her mother's family. Like many Irish men in the mid-Victorian period, her maternal grandfather, James MacSherry, a Catholic, had emigrated to Middlesbrough and found work in the shipyards. Tragedy struck when he was working at a height, suspended over the side of a vessel, and the supporting rope gave way. There was intense hostility between Irish Catholics and Orangemen in the yards and, as Dorothy says, 'to her dying day' her grandmother swore that an enemy had deliberately cut the rope. She was left with three small children but no income. Yet with great tenacity she refused to compromise her independence by accepting charity. Uneducated and completely illiterate, she had one highly marketable talent. She was a superb cook and affluent families vied for her services which brought in an income on which to support herself and her family.

Dorothy Stutt (née Gardam) in her early Twenties. (Dorothy Stutt)

One daughter, Alice, took up hotel work in Stockton, and it was there that she met her future husband, Herbert Gardam, a Protestant, whose family came from Hull. Their marriage produced one child, Dorothy, who is now Dorothy Stutt.

Herbert Gardam returned to Hull with his wife and daughter and settled in a house off Spring Street, not far from St. Patrick's church, the focus of so much of the lives of the family, including that of Herbert himself, a quiet, reserved man who was very fond of music and loved the singing at Mass and Benediction. His wife never pressed him to change his religion but this came about, indirectly, through one of his secular pleasures, playing billiards with another aficionado of the game, Father Alphonsus Wannyn ('a lovely priest', according to Dorothy). In the First World War Herbert was conscripted into the army and, just before he left, Father Wannyn made the suggestion: 'Before you go, Herbert, how about becoming a Catholic?' It was an opportune moment. Mr. Gardam took Father Wannyn's advice, and followed his adopted faith with great devotion and sincerity for the rest of his life.

Dorothy loved St. Patrick's and took particular delight in the Latin of the Liturgy. As a budding writer, she was always sensitive to language, and the sound of spoken or sung Latin gave her great pleasure. The change to the vernacular in the wake of Vatican II was one reform she disliked. At St. Patrick's there were name plates indicating rented seats, but Dorothy liked to see what was going on and always walked to the front, ignoring such reservations. For a short time she was persuaded to join the choir but soon decided this was absurd as she could not sing a note, and quickly resigned. 'Dolly, why are you no longer in the choir?' the priest, Canon James Barry, enquired. 'Because I'm neither use nor ornament,' she replied. 'I don't know about ornament,' said Canon Barry, both diplomatically and gallantly.

The Catechism had, of course, to be learnt by heart, and there were sections which were difficult for a child to master, but, once assimilated in this way, it was remembered for ever, and the resulting red letter day was her first Communion, when she was appropriately dressed and carried a beautiful white prayer book with gold clasps. Then, after the religious ceremony, came 'a splendid breakfast' provided by ladies of the parish. Fasting was always strictly observed: it was an irksome duty at times, but accepted without protest as a normal part of one's religious practice.

Another highlight was the May Day procession, when girls of the parish, all wearing white dresses, took their veils to church and then struggled to put them on in the only accommodation available, the confined spaces of the confessional boxes. The priest carried the monstrance and strewed flowers from a basket as he slowly walked the church's interior. Then the procession moved out into the streets where onlookers, no doubt appreciating the free and colourful spectacle, were, as Dorothy remembers, always respectful. She thinks, though, that such walks were not as common in Hull as they were in the towns of the West Riding.

Canon Barry's reputation was not restricted to his own parish. Contradicting the stereotyped image of the hard-drinking Irish priest, he was strictly teetotal, and, when he hosted his annual Christmas party for members of the choir, he provided every drink possible for his guests but drank no alcohol himself. On the night before he died, Dorothy's mother had an awful dream in which she saw St. Patrick's church draped in black and purple. Canon Barry was a great man for the outdoor, and the following morning he shouted 'Goodbye, Alice!' as he passed her in the street, biking out of Hull to take part in hare-coursing. She never saw him again. Later that day, while out in the country, he dropped down dead. It was a terrible shock to everyone, and, again in Dorothy's own words, 'the whole of Hull', people of every denomination, turned out for his funeral.

It was a time when many priests visited weekly, both for pastoral reasons and for collecting money, sometimes asked for but usually expected, even if not mentioned. Dorothy recalls one family being regularly followed-up for their absences from church and hearing the hammering on their door to bring out the recalcitrant parishioners.

St. Patrick's was very much a family church and its members tended to be clannish and form their own social set. There were affluent members, some well-known in Hull Catholic circles, who lived in the larger houses on Spring Bank or in the Avenues and with the means to be generous benefactors to the church. Through the kindness of Con O'Kelly, the boxer turned priest, St. Patrick's had acquired beautiful Stations of the Cross and a pulpit in Connemara marble.

But St. Patrick's was almost in the centre of Hull, and by far the larger number of parishioners were poor – probably 70% of them in Dorothy's opinion. Immigrant Italians formed a quasi-ghetto, and Mill Street was noted as an enclave of Catholics, particularly those of Irish origin. She remembers the Aldabella's, who kept a shop, and their daughter, Mary, who had the most beautiful voice. Church congregations delighted in her singing, and wealthy people would invite her to sing at their private social gatherings. The Collingwoods were one of the middle-class families with members professionally employed as bankers and lawyers, the Conlons were well-known tailors, and other names which come to mind are Hirst and Wrigglesworth.

Unexpectedly, Dorothy rejects the idea that there was greater anti-Catholic prejudice in the past. Some people, she thinks, have that attitude now, as they did then, but otherwise she is not conscious of any fundamental difference, though she accepts that official cooperation between different denominations is far more evident today.

Apart from a short period at St. Patrick's, the Catholic school in Mill Street, and the time when she was living in South Bank, all her education was at the Convent on Anlaby Road. At first her mother paid her fees but later Dorothy won a scholarship, and tuition in the senior department was free. The Convent school was run by Sisters of Mercy and there was noticeable rivalry with the French Convent, where the Canonesses of St. Augustine exuded a certain air of social superiority and where the timetable, which included needlework and other refined accomplishments, was more suited to girls from richer families who were destined to become ladies and did not need the academic grounding doled out by the Sisters of Mercy to their pupils. Educational standards, Dorothy claims, were much higher at her school and she had no option but to learn the subjects drummed into her. A Proustian memory, which remains as pungent as it did when it attacked her nostrils all those years ago, is of the appalling smell of the soup served at midday to boarders.

The Anlaby Road Convent had a number of nuns still vividly recalled almost a century later as 'horrors', and, even among these Sisters, there was a degree of snobbery which caused great pain to a girl from a relatively poor home. Mrs. Gardam could not afford to buy the regulation gymslip demanded by the nuns, and sent Dorothy to school in a home-made version. Both the rather flashy gym mistress and one of the nuns sneered when they saw Dorothy wearing this inferior garment, and the memory of the pain they caused has stayed with her. 'Snobbishness at that age hurts like hell,' she comments in her customary forthright way. One Sister, still remembered by name but in this context charitably left anonymous, she recalls as 'an aristocratic horror' who taught badly and whose art lessons consisted of having her pupils draw endless pictures of flowers in vases. She remembers, too, the fuss made over a girl whose father was a director of a large store: disappointingly, the nuns tended to behave in this way when they had hopes of obtaining goods at bargain prices.

But there were compensations, for schooldays are usually a mixture of contrasting experiences. Her favourite subject was English and she loved Mrs. Carter, 'a dear little woman', who taught so well. The convent itself had a quiet charm and Dorothy loved to watch the nuns walking slowly round the cloister reading their breviaries, an oasis of peace in a busy city.

There were visits to St. Charles, where she was overawed by the beauty of the ceiling, but irreverent thoughts mingled with her imagination as the shape of the orb rising majestically above the altar always made her think of the more familiar hambone.

Dorothy met her future husband, Edwin Stutt, a member of an old Catholic family, whose father and uncle (then called Stutz) had come to England from Bavaria. Edwin's father had caused a deep rift by marrying a Scottish Protestant (though she later became Catholic), an offence which resulted in his being ostracised by the rest of the family. The Stutts were in shipping in Newcastle, and Edwin had originally been articled to a shipbroker, but a slump in the industry brought him to Hull to take up a post with a firm of tobacco merchants. It was a marriage which united two different strands of Catholic history, and provided one more example of the rich and complex genealogical inheritance of Catholics who would always describe themselves as very ordinary.